CW00596939

SPECIAL EDUCATION SERIES
Peter Knoblock, Editor

Helping the Visually Impaired Child with Developmental Problems

Effective Practice in Home, School, and Community

Sally M. Rogow

Teachers College, Columbia University
New York and London

Published by Teachers College Press, 1234 Amsterdam Avenue,
New York, NY 10027

Library of Congress Cataloging-in-Publication Data

Rogow, Sally M. (Sally Muriel), 1930–
  Helping the visually impaired child with developmental problems:
effective practice in home, school, and community / Sally M. Rogow.
    p. cm.—(Special education series ; 6)
  Bibliography: p.
  Includes index.
  ISBN 0-8077-2903-5.   ISBN 0-8077-2902-7 (pbk.)
  1. Visually handicapped children—Education—United States.
2. Developmentally disabled children—Education—United States.
3. Visually handicapped children—United States. 4. Developmentally
disabled children—United States. I. Title. II. Series: Special
education series (New York, N.Y.)
HV1795.R64   1988   88-2222
362.1'968—dc19   CIP

Manufactured in the United States of America

93 92 91 90 89 88   1 2 3 4 5 6

Contents

Preface

This book is about visually impaired children who are developmentally delayed or have additional developmental handicaps. The premise of the book is that interaction with people and the environment is essential to effective learning and personal growth. Blindness and severe visual handicaps restrict the ease of environmental interactions. Severe visual handicaps in combination with other developmental problems—whether neurological, sensory, physical, intellectual, or emotional—not only constrain, they may actually prevent children from having the normal environmental and social interactions that mediate learning. The developmental consequences of nonparticipation are devastating. Parents and teachers, presented with the passivity, resistance, and unreceptive stance of these children, face a monumental task in attempting to invite their participation. This book is written to contribute to the special education of these children; in the book they are called by fictitious names, but the children whose tales are told are very real and their stories are true.

The book is organized into nine chapters. The first chapter presents the dynamic interactionist model of intervention; this model is the basis for the structure and methodology utilized throughout the book. Chapter 1 also includes discussion of the conceptual and social issues surrounding the children and their families. In Chapter 2, the nature of intervention in infancy and early childhood and the implications of infant research on that intervention are examined.

The next two chapters familiarize readers with the visual impairments and learning capabilities of the children under consideration here. The nature and developmental consequences of visually handicapping conditions and of developmental and/or sensory handicaps that may be associated with them are described in Chapter 3. Chapter 4 explores body image, the notion of self, sensory integration, and hand development as these aspects of human development relate to sensorimotor learning and interaction within the physical environment. Methodologies based on music therapy and co-active movement theory are also reviewed in this chapter.

The chapters that follow discuss various educational interventions to assist in the development of the whole child. The overarching goal of any intervention is to enhance the child's social and environmental interactions. The applications of research on infant communication and early language development are examined in Chapter 5, which also includes descriptions of speech and language disorders and discussion of methodologies to encourage communicative responses. The relationships between play and social interaction are explored in Chapter 6. Additionally, techniques to develop exploratory and symbolic play are illustrated. Chapter 7 examines strategies for creating environmental awareness and establishing independence skills. Effective methods of teaching independent mobility to nonverbal and multiply handicapped children and young adults are also described. Finally, Chapter 8 explores the growing role of sophisticated electronic technology to assist with instruction and provide augmentative systems of communication.

The book concludes with an examination of the social interests of children and their families, the role learning environments play in children's social identities, and the importance of assisting with transitions to adulthood. Social policies and human services, both those currently in place and those still evolving, are discussed in light of the book's emphasis on social and environmental interaction. Community integration—in the home, school, and workplace—thus becomes the means as well as the end.

Acknowledgments

This book would not be complete without acknowledging the help of those who contributed so much to its content. First there are the teachers whose work contributed so much to the writing of this book. Some of the teachers were my students; all are esteemed colleagues who know how to quicken responsiveness and establish contact with the most recalcitrant of learners. Then there are the children who, by becoming active learners, illustrate the magic of the teaching/learning process. The children's parents, who gave us their trust, touched us deeply and gave meaning and significance to our work. In particular, I would like to express my gratitude to Mr. and Mrs. Howard Chu, from whom I learned so much about the parent experience and the need to believe in the educability of severely multiply impaired children.

This book would not have been possible without the encouragement of colleagues. Special acknowledgment is given to dear friend and colleague Berdell (Pete) Wurzburger, who generously shared his knowledge of teaching independent mobility to multiply handicapped blind children. I also gratefully acknowledge the encouragement and endless patience of my family: My husband, Robert, who with unfailing good humor read and reread these chapters and contributed enormously to the organization of the text, and my daughters—Fern, whose expertise as a speech pathologist contributed to the writing of the chapter on communication and language, and Andrea, who provided steady encouragement. I am also grateful for the encouragement, support, and assistance of the editors at Teachers College Press.

Helping the Visually Impaired Child with Developmental Problems

Effective Practice in Home, School, and Community

1.

Dynamic Interaction:
A Conceptual Framework

Meningitis at birth left Eddy totally blind and quadriplegic. Doctors predicted that the baby boy would be profoundly retarded and discouraged his adoptive parents from taking him home. Eddy seemed to be in pain for most of his first year, crying day and night. Nothing could soothe him. His parents were exhausted but they refused to give Eddy up. The adoption agency offered to annul the adoption and place the infant in a foster home. His parents refused and rejected their physician's view that Eddy's discomfort was due to his handicaps. They took the year-old boy from one specialist to another in the hope of discovering the cause of his pain. Their efforts were rewarded when an orthopedic specialist discovered that the infant had a dislocated hip that prevented him from finding a comfortable position.

After the hip was repaired, Eddy was transformed into a content and lovable baby who loved to cuddle. The progress of his development was painfully slow, but despite the delays, he was sociable and enjoyed interacting with members of his family. He recognized people from their voices and cooed, smiled, and laughed whenever he heard a familiar voice. When Eddy was 4 years old, his parents began to feel that he was trying to communicate with them verbally. Even though they could not understand his inarticulate sounds, they were sure he was saying something: His vocal noises sounded almost like speech. Eddy kept on trying to speak, and finally, just before his fifth birthday, he made himself understood. Gradually his articulation improved and by the age of six years, Eddy could speak clearly. It took longer for sentences to come, but by his seventh birthday Eddy could speak in well-formed sentences.

Too physically handicapped to have success with braille, Eddy learned to read with the help of the Fishburne alphabet, a non-braille tactile method of reading. The system is clumsy, but it allowed him to demonstrate his ability. Eddy attends a special program at a junior high school, doing academic work with the help of a computer, that he ac-

1

tivates with special switches. His computer has a speech output attachment.

Amanda is also congenitally blind, due to anophthalmia, a developmental anomaly. Feeding problems during her first year necessitated long periods of hospitalization; she did not eat solid foods until she was nearly five years old. Amanda did not vocalize, and there was the suspicion of brain damage and other associated anomalies, but her physical development was normal and she was physically active. She enjoyed music and movement and was far more interested in playing with water at the sink than playing with toys. At age four, Amanda displayed object behavior reminiscent of that of a much younger child—she enjoyed pulling objects out of bags or banging them together. Amanda, like Eddy, was responsive to adults and enjoyed physical movement. Although she seemed to understand what people said to her, Amanda did not speak until she was five years of age, whereupon she immediately began speaking in phrases and sentences. Amanda is attending kindergarten and receives special instruction from the teachers in the resource room for visually impaired children in a public school setting.

Robby has some sight but is legally blind. He was born two months prematurely and has epilepsy but no physical handicap. The first two months of his life were spent in an incubator. His sight problem is due to congenital cataracts. Robby's natural mother could not bring him home from the hospital and Robby was placed in a series of foster homes. As an infant, he had feeding and sleeping problems. Robby has always received good physical care, but since he always resisted being hugged or cuddled, he was never able to form close attachments to other people. In addition to making him hard to reach, his withdrawn and resistant behavior discouraged others from developing a sense of closeness to him. He liked being left alone to listen to a radio.

At eight years of age, Robby spoke clearly but did not converse with anyone. He contented himself with repeating the words of television commercials or snatches of other people's conversation. His performance in gross and fine motor tasks was poor; his hands seemed limp and lifeless. He stubbornly clung to routines and rejected efforts to engage him in group activities. Robby was a solitary and sad little boy, deeply engrossed in a private world. His only skill was his language, which tended to be overlooked because he seemed so "tuned out."

He was finally placed with foster parents who viewed Robby as a challenge. They spent a great deal of time with him; he was taken on outings, talked to, and given responsibility around the house—in short, he was expected to act like a "regular eight-year-old kid." Slowly the chinks in his protective armor grew and his rigidity began to wear away; the personality of a delightful and talented child began to make its appearance. Close cooperation between home and school effected other dramatic changes. Robby now goes to a secondary school.

This book is about children like Eddy, Amanda, and Robby. It is an optimistic book because it is about children learning, about their humanity, and about the wellsprings of growth that lie beneath handicap. These children show us that there are various pathways to optimal learning and effective social functioning.

The author has been engaged for the past twenty years in preparing teachers for the challenging and rewarding work of special education of blind, visually impaired, and visually impaired/multiply handicapped children.

The behavior of children reveals their inner worlds: their fears, their confusions, their talents and abilities. They have much to teach about the nature of learning and mental growth. The dedication of their parents and teachers to fire the tiniest sparks of initiative inspired this book. The purpose of this book is to share what the children have taught us about themselves, about learning, and about the ingredients of the teaching and learning process.

This chapter will introduce the philosophy and perspectives that have given form to the ideas to be discussed in the text and introduce the issues that surround the education and treatment of visually impaired children who have developmental problems.

A Perspective on the Development
of Handicapped Children

Children like Eddy, Amanda, and Robby achieve social competence when they are valued and treated as capable of learning. Perceptions of self, healthy or otherwise, mirror the perceptions held by others: Children only learn to believe in themselves when the people closest to them have faith in their abilities to learn. When children begin to make sense of their physical and social worlds, they can start to interact with those worlds in meaningful and important ways (M. Donaldson, 1978).

When they are neglected or not expected to learn, children like Eddy, Amanda, and Robby are easily misjudged and devalued. The parameters of normal development, based on the sequences of growth observed in nonhandicapped children, may not be relevant to visually impaired children, especially those with additional handicaps.

The goal of education for handicapped children is the achievement of competence, which can take a variety of forms. One kind of competence is mastery over the physical environment, which includes movement, locomotion, mobility, and manipulation of objects. Another type is communicative competence, the ability to understand, respond, and effectively represent one's needs, wants, and ideas to other people. Social competence describes the capacity to adapt, adjust, and function in society. In general, competence is the ability of the individual to act in goal-directed ways and to communicate, interact, and comfortably adapt within a social environment. Interaction within the social and physical world is the means by which competence develops. The activities of children as they interact with their social and physical worlds, beginning at the moment of birth, are the pathways to growth in understanding, thought, and behavior (Tinbergen & Tinbergen, 1983). Disabilities and handicaps, particularly in combination, are obstacles to development because they curtail the freedom to explore and achieve contact with the environment.

Children like Eddy cannot learn to control the physical aspects of interaction without special help. For example, the action of reaching for and handling an object requires ability both to control the hand and arm and to synchronize movement. Eddy lacks the necessary motor ability, and his visual impairment deprives him of important sensory information that would help him coordinate the movements that he can make. Eddy's situation stands in marked contrast to that of a nonhandicapped child. In normal development, an intact and efficient nervous system, unimpeded by sensory or neurological handicap, permits a high level of sensorimotor integration. The seeing child simultaneously sees, hears, and feels. Sensory integration, which seems to occur so easily and naturally in nonhandicapped children, needs to be carefully nurtured in handicapped children. For example, blind children must learn to use their hands to substitute for their eyes to achieve contact with the physical world. They must learn to associate the sounds they hear with real objects before sound alone can convey information about the events happening around them. Sensation that is not integrated with meaning tends to be fragmentary and disembodied. The soundscape of the world is uninforming until sound is linked to its sources. Sound alone can only convey information when it is associated with the people and objects producing sounds. Blind children hear footsteps, doors opening and closing, wind blowing, birds singing, but until they know something about the objects and events around them, they attach little meaning to what they hear. Associations between sounds and people and objects come about with repeated experience. Only the sense of sight gives immediate information about the environment. Physical and/ or neurological handicaps, even mild ones, in combination with visual impairments place many constraints on one's ability to learn about the world.

Tinbergen and Tinbergen (1983) in their discussion of disturbed behavior observed that it is not just the child himself who is malfunctioning: "What is actually ill is something larger: the child in the web of his relationships with the social and physical outside world" (p. 21). The failure to establish social bonds is sometimes the most pervasive characteristic of developmentally delayed blind children. Robby's behavior expressed his inability to form close human attachments with other people. He resisted being held and kept his environment from intruding on his life. Without intimate connections to other people, there is a tragic failure of human bonding. Social interaction is the source of human learning and human growth; its absence leaves the child bereft of social models and social connections that are the core of the developmental process. Inability to reach out to the environment results in secondary behavioral problems that devastate the development of meaningful relationships with others. Behavioral difficulties can be treated with social interventions that increase the individual's ability to communicate and interact with the environment. Dysfunctional children must be seen as capable of learning and relating to the world in goal-oriented ways. Some of the children described in this book spent years like rudderless ships drifting in the seas of time and space, until finally someone recognized and nurtured their abilities.

The potential of human adaptability is nowhere more evident than in the course of the development of children with complex handicaps. Edward Mysak (1980), the noted speech scientist, observed that the development of handicapped children does not need to duplicate that of nonhandicapped children, and its differences do not make it inferior. Children may show adequate coping skills in some areas and severe deficits in others.

Issues in the Education of Handicapped Children

One of the important issues in special education is how to apply developmental research to the education of handicapped children. Research in the neurosciences has much to teach about the capacities of the human brain to compensate for injuries to nervous pathways. Research in infant development has illuminated the nature of human interdependency and the role of caregivers in promoting human learning. Human infants thrive within a social context of affectionate caregiving. An appreciation of the role of caregivers in the development of children can lead to the creation of instructional procedures that encourage and support interaction and reciprocal responding.

Philosophical frameworks, be they psychodynamic, developmental, or behavioral, are made explicit by the organization of instruction and the methods employed; but philosophical frameworks are not the whole story. They are abstractions far removed from the day-to-day interactions between children and teachers, and it is the quality of these interactions that determine the success of learning and teaching.

Transactions with Children

A dynamic interactionist model of human growth and learning provides the framework for the interventions discussed in this book. This model of learning is based on the belief that the transactions that take place between children and their environments shape the learning that takes place. Growth and learning are continuous processes involving conscious awareness and response, adaptation, and judgment. (Stern, 1977). Normal infant development demonstrates the importance of interaction in shaping awareness and responsiveness.

Insights from Infant Development.   Researchers studying infants in their natural context are seeing infants "as new human beings with an evolutionary heritage of social interdependency and as social people who already possess the ability to influence and be influenced by others" (Tronick & Adamson, 1980, p. 162). Minute by minute recordings of infant behavior, made possible by television technology, are revealing the subtle processes of human interactions. By studying social interaction in slow motion, tiny units of behavior are revealing the competence of infants in communicating with their worlds. As Brazelton (1977) noted, human infants have a long period of childhood dependency in which to learn to survive and utilize all of their potential for learning and thinking. How they do this depends on the experiences they have with the world around them.

Brazelton (1977) ascribes the development of children to three powerful forces. The first is the growth and maturation of the central nervous system. The second force comes from within and consists of individual genetic influences. The third force is provided by parents and other nurturing people within the environment. Each developmental step is achieved systematically. Feedback from success in one step leads to the next and nourishes an inner "sense of competence." The three main elements of the developmental process are (1) infants' biological equipment for dealing with their environments, (2) the environments, and (3) the nature of the interaction between infants and their environments.

Almost from the moment of birth, infants seek stimulation and action and actively participate in interactions with their environments (Stern, 1977). Within a few weeks after birth, babies are signaling their interest in the actions of adults with their smiles, their eyes, their hands, and the positions of their heads. Brazelton (1977) noted that behavior is the infant's principal means of communication. Through a process of mutual modification, mothers and infants establish patterns of relating (Packer & Rosenblatt, 1979).

Stern (1977) made an extensive study of the relationships of mothers and infants and concluded that in the first few weeks and months of life, infants become expert at "maintaining and modulating the flow of a social exchange" (p. 1). He called these social exchanges "biologically designed choreography" and hypothesized that they are prototypes of later interpersonal exchanges. The social nature of the infant's world fuels the drive toward growth and learning. Through interactions with their parents, infants gain entry into their society and culture.

Caregiving adults behave in ways that enable infants to learn social behaviors. Adult actions model behaviors that infants learn to imitate. Imitation itself is communication and a strategy for learning about oneself and one's relations with the world. Mothers exaggerate facial expressions and postures of head and body that engage the attention of infants and help them organize their perceptions. For example, the mother makes facial expressions while vocalizing and looking, thus providing the infant with a multi-modal event. The infant experiences the event as a single unit, a coordinated package (Stern, 1977). Stern noted that the perception of a multi-modal event as a single unit may be the basis of sensory integration.

The readiness of infants to participate in social interaction depends on their abilities to perceive and maintain attention to sensory stimuli (Packer & Rosenblatt, 1979). Nature has given infants the ability to select the sensory stimuli that are experienced as comfortable and to reject those that are uncomfortable. Infants close their eyes to bright white light, but become alert and look intently at red or soft yellow objects dangled in front of them. Quieting and alerting responses are more consistently observed as reactions to soft, high-pitched voices than to low ones. Babies find touch and gentle pressure on parts of their bodies to be soothing. Fussing babies quiet when a hand is placed on the abdomen (Brazelton, 1977). Swaddling is an old remedy for fussy babies because infants find a steady touch soothing. The infant is constantly receiving and reacting to sensory stimulation. With each stimulus reaction, the infant brain is storing experiences for future learning (Brazelton, 1977). In normal development, there is a mutual adaptability—a ''fit''—between the infant and the environment that suggests that infants are biologically prepared to respond to the environment.

The brain is dependent on the external world for the information it receives. Eyes, ears, hands, and other body parts convey sense impressions to the brain, which does the real work of perceiving. Sensory systems, whether they serve vision, hearing, touch, or other sensations, appear to work in fundamentally similar ways to code the vast arrays of stimuli into a highly organized and sensible experience of the world (Ornstein & Thompson, 1984).

As Als, Tronick, and Brazelton (1980) noted, the growth and maturation of the nervous system determines the course of development. When the ability of the nervous system to receive and utilize information is not intact, the course of development is disrupted. The flow of sensation to the brain may be blocked by inability of the eye, ear, hand, or other body part to detect sensation, or by injured nerve pathways that do not carry sensation to the brain, or a combination of both. The precise nature of the interference may be difficult to identify. Development in some children seems painfully slow, especially in the early years; in others it seems to have been arrested, and in still others it appears grossly uneven and distorted. The course of impaired development will perhaps be better understood with more knowledge of the workings of the brain itself.

Insights from the Neurosciences. There is evidence to suggest that the nervous system has some built-in reserves. These reserves give the nervous system flexibility or plasticity. Gardner (1983) identified five principles that appear to govern the plasticity of the nervous system. The first principle concerns the flexibility of the nervous system. Studies by neurobiologists seem to confirm that during the earliest periods of life the nervous system can adapt flexibly to severe injury. Nerve cells collect and form alternate routes or pathways if the injury occurs early enough. Research evidence has shown that even in the face of severe injury, learning can proceed almost unimpeded (Gardner, 1983).

The second principle concerns the notion of critical periods for learning. During these critical periods rapid learning occurs if the proper conditions exist (Gardner, 1983). For example, the best time for language acquisition is within early childhood; after that period, language is far more difficult to acquire and may be learned differently (Fromkin, Krashen, Curtiss, Rigler, & Rigler 1974).

A third principle concerns the differing degrees of flexibility from region to region within the brain. According to Gardner, regions of the brain that develop later in childhood, such as the frontal lobes, turn out to be more malleable than the primary sensory cortex, which develops earlier. Language may be unaffected in children who have sustained massive injury or even removal of an entire hemisphere of the brain in the first few years of life (Gardner, 1983). This remarkable fact suggests that large portions of the brain (the cortex) remain uncommitted and are thus available for compensation.

The fourth principle holds that organisms will not develop properly unless they have certain experiences. For example, cats will have faulty vision if they are not exposed to patterned light after birth or if they are prevented from using both eyes and moving about. If one eye is covered, the cat will not learn to use the other. If proper stimulation is not available, developmental goals will not be achieved (Gardner, 1983).

The fifth principle is concerned with the long-term effects of injury to the nervous system. Some injuries have immediate effects, while others are invisible at first and make their appearance later in the child's life. The human nervous system's plasticity and ability to compensate may explain why development in some children seems to be so slow in the early years and then speeds up. This highlights the importance of sensory stimulation in infancy and suggests that multiple handicaps do not inevitably lead to severe forms of mental retardation.

The Effects of Blindness on Interaction in Infancy.   Ease of interaction with the environment is constrained by visual handicaps, even in the absence of other disabilities. One effect of blindness is its impact on caregivers. Mothers of blind infants wonder if their babies really know them. Visual regard plays so central a role in human engagement that it is natural to attribute "knowing" and "recognition" to visual behavior.

Fraiberg (1979) observed that the effect of loss of visual regard is difficult to overcome, simply because visual regard is part of the universal human code of the human fraternity: "When the eyes do not meet ours in acknowledgement of our presence, it feels curiously like a rebuff" (p. 155).

In the presence of serious handicap, parents are simultaneously trying to cope with and adjust to the needs of their babies while dealing with their own feelings of grief and anxiety. The early development of handicapped infants is made even more complicated by prematurity, extended hospitalization, early feeding problems, and the necessity for prolonged medical treatment. Difficulties in establishing mutuality of responsiveness with their infants contribute to parental anxiety and frustration. On the other hand, when parents know how to help their children, they are more likely to relax and face the difficulties ahead with assurance (Als, Tronick, & Brazelton, 1980). Intervention during the infant years should be a source of strength and encouragement to parents.

Social Issues

The social issues surrounding children with severe handicaps concern their families, their treatment, and their futures. Recognition of the essential human needs of children and their families has been slow in coming. Physicians, teachers, and therapists come and go. Some get to know the children well, while others only see the child occasionally. Parents must keep a constant vigil, learn to take pride in small but steady steps, keep their hopes alive, and take disappointment in stride.

As the family's need for supportive services and the handicapped child's right to treatment and education tailored to individual needs (not diagnostic categories) have begun to be addressed, a third issue—the right to live in the community—has emerged. It arises from a recognition that the settings in which the child's daily life, education, and treatment take place play an important role in both quality of life and eventual outcome. Three concepts implied by this right—normalization, integration, and deinstitutionalization—have become important forces in the revolution in the treatment of children with multiple handicaps.

Societal values, public policy, government funding, community involvement, family support, and individual effort are among the multitude of influences that are brought to bear on these issues, and their effects are often interdependent and reciprocal. It is therefore important to examine the social implications of handicapping conditions in some detail and to gain an understanding of their complications and ramifications.

The Needs of Families.   Children's families are their most important resource: Children must live within families if they are to be part of human culture, for culture is transmitted through family life. Language, social relationships, styles of social interaction, dress, and a thousand other aspects of cultural participation are best learned within the context of family living. No professional service can replace parents in the day-to-day care of children, but outside help must be available if families are to maintain their children within the home and provide the level of care needed.

Support services that enable parents to cope with the multiple needs of their children include: architectural modifications to the home, counseling/therapeutic services, child care assistance, homemaker services, in-home training for parents, respite care, transportation, and access to specialized equipment and medical services. Family supports are built on the assumption that families themselves are the experts on what services they will need to support their children in their own homes (Bersani, 1987).

The birth of a child with complex handicaps places families in a position of dependence on public and private agencies. Their reliance on a variety of medical, educational, and social service personnel becomes a fact of their lives. Too often parents find themselves in conflict with physicians and other professionals. Although few professionals would deny the importance of parent involvement, parents are sometimes cast in the role of passive observers, rather than active participants in making the decisions that affect the lives of their children. Parents need practical support in their communities; they need information about available services and how to enlist them. A network of cooperating agencies can serve families far better than single agencies that deal with only a portion of a family's and a child's needs.

Systems of Classifying Children.   Labels that carry hopeless and pessimistic prognoses discourage parents and may prevent children from receiving services. No child should be labeled "severely" or "profoundly" retarded when very young or before there have been opportunities for stimulation and intervention. Hopeless labels rarely lead to consistent and intensive intervention; they dehumanize and isolate children and their families. Blind and other visually impaired children are often misdiagnosed and set adrift in systems in which their needs are obscured. Hobbs (1980) stated that labels should be functional and should link the child and the family to needed services. Medical, psychological and educational assessment should be used to develop "service plans," not to classify children into disability categories.

Children like Eddy, Amanda, and Robby all have severe visual problems, but they are uniquely individual. The complexity of their developmental problems cautions against the use of simplistic methods of assessing, classifying, or teaching them. Traditional single-handicap approaches do not serve the needs of these children.

Mental retardation is regarded in this book as a symptom and not a cause of low levels of function in blind children. Gold (1980) provided a functional definition of mental retardation that is useful in planning for children.

> Mental retardation refers to a level of functioning which requires from society significantly above average training procedures and superior assets in adaptive behavior on the part of society, manifested throughout the life of both society and the individual. (p. 5)

Gold's definition suggests the relationship between the retarded person's level of function and the availability of education, treatment, and the resources society is willing to allocate. Gold also considers maladaptive behavior to be caused by environments in which the personal and social needs of children are not being met. Prolonged frustration leads to disturbed and maladaptive behavior and not to some condition that exists within the child. As Gold (1980) observed, all children are capable of adaptive behavior. Behavior does not define potential.

Right to Treatment.   In a true sense we can measure the humanity of any society by the treatment it accords its handicapped members. Recognition and implementation of the rights of handicapped children to life-sustaining treatment—rights that are not clearly articulated in law or policy—have become an issue that is most dramatically seen in the case of handicapped infants. As enormous advances in medical technology have increased treatment options for handicapped infants, decisions regarding withholding treatment have come to depend more and more on a host of nonmedical factors.

Magnet and Kluge (1987) reviewed current practices about how decisions are made and who is making them in North American hospitals. In some places defective newborns are denied life-saving surgeries without consultation with parents. Magnet and Kluge (1987) argue that parents should be fully and accurately informed about their child's condition. Medical expertise and authority should be confined to technical and prognostic questions. A very fine line exists between withholding medical attention and actively causing the death of the infant.

Recognizing the grave danger inherent in society's acceptance of refusing medical treatment to handicapped infants, parents' groups have opposed arbitrary decisions to withhold medical treatment from handicapped children. In cooperation with the American Academy of Pediatrics, a set of principles governing the treatment of disabled infants was prepared in 1983. Included in them is the statement that the presence of handicap must not be allowed to determine decisions concerning medical care.

Rejecting the notion of handicap as disease, the parents of handicapped children have assumed an active role in securing education and treatment. The parent movement gained momentum in the late 1950s in the wake of the civil rights movement. Primarily as a result of parent efforts, the rights of handicapped children to education and treatment have been written into law, specifically the "Education for All Children Act" of 1975.

It was not so very long ago that there were few alternatives for families; lack of practical support within the community forced many families to place their children into institutions (Oswin, 1978). The parent movement has succeeded in bringing about radical changes in both education and treatment. Most jurisdictions in North America are at least offering some services to help families stay together (Bersani, 1987). Family supports are effective and reduce the need for out-of-home placements.

Parents consider the human needs of their children to be just as important as their special needs. Parents of multiply impaired children, as stated in a brief prepared by British Columbians for Mentally Handicapped Persons (1986), want their "sons and daughters to be able to live with style, comfort, safety, and dignity and to carry on with the business of living, working, having fun, and participating in the lives of their communities, as we all do" (p. 3). The brief further states that handicapped children have the right to "live with and not apart from their families, friends, and neighbors" (p. 3).

Normalization.   The concept of normalization was first articulated in 1969 by Bank Mikkelson, director of the Danish Mental Retardation Service (Wolfensberger, 1972). Mikkelson advocated that mentally retarded people be allowed to live according to the patterns and rhythms of life in the mainstream of society. Normalization means just that: The conditions of living characteristic of a society's nonhandicapped population should be accorded to its handicapped people.

Normalization is deceptively simple in its formulation and complex in its application, for it affects not only handicapped persons but also the interactions between handicapped and nonhandicapped people in society. Its implementation involves the entire system of management of handicapped persons (Wolfensberger, 1972). By focusing on the human need to "belong" and "have a place in society," the principle of normalization forces examination of the environments society creates for handicapped people. Its focus is on the individual, the immediate and primary social system (e.g., family, peer group, school), and the larger society, especially its laws and mores. The principle of normalization has already made an enormous contribution to improving education and treatment. Policies based on the principle shift the focus from concern with the characteristics of handicapping conditions to efforts to improve the quality of environments by working with families and service systems (Wolfensberger, 1972).

Integration.   As Wolfensberger (1972) has noted, "Ultimately, integration is only meaningful if it is social integration; i.e. if it involves social interaction and acceptance, and not merely physical presence" (p. 48). Thus the essence of integration is inclusion of handicapped persons by their communities. *Mainstreaming* is the term applied to the inclusion of handicapped children in community schools, where they have opportunities to interact with their nonhandicapped peers. By precluding the education of children in closed or segregated settings, the principle of integration opens their education to public scrutiny and investigation and thus improves its quality. Integrated education, based on careful planning and parent participation, has improved both the delivery and the quality of educational services. Integration will be more fully discussed in Chapter 9.

Deinstitutionalization and Community Participation.   Deinstitutionalization is the movement toward community-based services and away from large, segregated, isolated institutions. Community participation is the development of programs and services for handicapped people within their home communities. Community participation is an extension of the original notion of deinstitutionalization, which is simply the relocation of services into smaller, less isolated settings. Community participation places emphasis on bridging the gaps between the demands of the environment and the abilities of handicapped people (Knoll & Ford, 1987).

Parents want their children to live where they can see them often so they may keep them within the circle of family life. Group homes within communities meet the needs of young adults and their families. The best residential arrangements are small group homes in which handicapped young people can feel secure and experience control over their environments; this is not possible in large institutions.

Normalization, integration, and deinstitutionalization have revolutionized the delivery of services to disabled children and their families. Current social policies reflect these philosophies. Ultimately, however, the social interests of children and their families are served by people, not social policies. Humane and responsive social policies create a climate of caring, but human services are delivered by the physicians, teachers, therapists, social workers, and others who serve the child and family. Compensatory education and habilitation alone are not sufficient to meet the social interests of children and their families. Human development is a social process and occurs within the social context of the family, the school, and society.

Summary

The integrating theme of this book is the importance of social and environmental interaction in relation to all domains of learning. All forms of learning are dependent on environmental contexts. As Piaget (1962) has asserted, there is continuity between the simplest kinds of adaptive behavior and highly evolved forms of intelligence. One grows out of the other. The roots of all forms of knowledge reside in action. Piaget has repeatedly observed that learning is an active process of construction. Knowledge does not come from the outside; it is fashioned by the mind in the course of active interaction with the social and physical worlds.

Gardner (1983) defined intelligence as "the ability to solve problems, to create products, that are valued among one or more cultural settings" (p. x). This definition argues against simplistic concepts of learning and intelligence. Some types of learning are made more difficult by the presence of a visual handicap, especially when it occurs in combination with other disabilities. The goal of education is the nurturance of the mind; the role of the educator is to find ways to stimulate, coax, and encourage mental development.

2.

Intervention in Infancy and Early Childhood

Progress in the education and treatment of handicapped infants can be measured by changes in attitudes and expectations, more sophisticated means of identification and treatment, and a framework of support services available to families. Advances in infant research are shedding light on the processes of learning in infancy and helping to shape new strategies of intervention.

The purpose of this chapter is to examine the social and conceptual issues of intervention in infancy. The preceding chapter introduced the theme of social interaction and the conceptual and social policy issues in relation to education and treatment; in this chapter these issues will be discussed in relation to infants and their families, in particular the needs of visually impaired infants and their families, and research in infant development and its implications for early intervention.

The primary aim of early intervention is to help parents establish early environmental interactions. Social, emotional, and mental development begin with birth. Intervention in infancy has a record of proven effectiveness: Well-planned interventions strengthen and enrich emotional attachments between parent and child; interventions in the form of services to families encourage parents, provide them with the knowledge and skills to help their own infants, and thus help to prevent secondary handicaps associated with understimulation.

Early intervention helps children get off to a good start, but it is not a panacea that solves all problems. As Clarke and Clarke (1979) noted, belief in the formative effects of the early years has led to an exaggerated belief that if all goes well in the first years of life, all will continue to go well. All the years of childhood are important. Early intervention does not replace later interventions, although it can help to prevent some developmental problems. Some handicapped infants take longer to respond. Slow beginnings should not alarm parents or discourage persistence. A history of early adversity in the infant years does not mean that the child will never be able to respond or that intervention should stop (Clarke & Clarke, 1979). Many children cannot express the knowledge they have absorbed until they have developed a means of communication.

Studies of young infants demonstrate their active role in initiating, and even creating the conditions of, their own learning. An infinite variety of infant/environment interactions stimulate growth and learning. Infant research is revealing the intricacies of these early interactions. Such studies hold important implications for early intervention, although visually impaired infants may not be replicating the same course of development as seen in sighted children (Warren, 1984).

A compelling reason for reviewing infant research is that the stages and sequences of normal development are frequently used as parameters to gauge the development of handicapped children. Developmental norms for nonhandicapped infants are used both as a basis for diagnosis and to identify objectives against which to measure progress (Walker & Crawley, 1983). Intervention programs are often based on the developmental sequences found in normal development, on the assumption that the developmental goals for handicapped children should be the same as those for their nonhandicapped peers. The advantage to this approach is that development as observed in normal infancy provides guidelines to the sequences of growth. However, the assumption that visually impaired children can or will follow nonhandicapped developmental sequences is problematic at best, because vision plays so central a role in early learning that its absence (in whole or in part) cannot help disrupting and altering the course of development.

Alternate paths to developmental goals must be taken by infants with sensory and physical handicaps. The heterogeneity of children with visual handicaps makes it extremely difficult to develop norms for this population. Observing the process of infant development and the interactions of children with their environments produces a far more useful guide to intervention than does assessment based on milestones of development. For example, standing alone is a milestone behavior, but before it can be achieved there is a great deal of unseen development that must take place in bones, muscles, and nerve pathways. Descriptions of behavior are rarely explanations of behavior.

Development in Infancy

Als, Tronick, and Brazelton (1980) proposed a model of development that incorporates the relationships between physiological development and sensorimotor development. Their model includes a hierarchy of four levels of organization; each new level of the hierarchy is established on the preceding level. At *Level 1,* infants gain control over basic physiological states such as heart rate, temperature control, respiration, and states of alertness. At *Level 2,* infants maintain a state of alertness and increase their repertoire of attending behaviors, such as orientation of face and head so that the eyes, face, and head are directed towards their mothers. These behaviors communicate interest and attention. *Level 3* of the hierarchy incorporates increased control of bodily postures and involvement of hands, arms, and head in mutual play with an adult. *Level 4* is characterized by the incorporation of toys and other objects in interactions with adults (Als, Tronick, & Brazelton, 1980).

As infants become more competent in interacting with their mothers, mothers become more competent in interpreting the actions of their infants. The steady drive toward increasingly complex behavior comes from both the actions of infants and and the responding behaviors of parents (Tronick & Adamson, 1980). Infant and mother help one another's developmental progression by supplying the feedback that completes each cycle.

Physiological States and Readiness

Readiness to interact with the environment is determined by physiological state. Infants who are unable to maintain an alert state for more than a few minutes at a time are not able to respond consistently to environmental stimuli. Rose (1983) reported that pre-term infants show less behavioral responsiveness to tactile stimuli than full-term babies. She noted that it was unclear whether pre-term infants have a higher threshhold for stimulation, cannot maintain vigorous responding, or a combination of the two.

Damage to the nervous system before, during, or immediately after birth may mean months of delay before the infant is able to respond consistently to external stimuli. In a study of the visual responses of pre-term infants, Sigman (1983) found that the more premature infants and those with more complicated medical conditions demonstrated much briefer visual fixations than either full-term infants or those with few complications. Sigman concluded that longer fixation durations reflect better physiological integration. Another important finding of this study is that there seemed to be a significant relationship between caregiver behaviors and infant visual fixation.

Attention to sensory stimulation is governed by the organization of the nervous system. Organized reflex patterns permit newborns to monitor and regulate the amount of sensation that can be handled. Brazelton (1977) noted that much of the complicated behavior of humans can be anticipated in early infancy in the form of reflexes. After the appearance of these complicated reflexes, they seem to go underground and return as controlled voluntary behavior.

Reflexes are, by definition, responses to stimulation, but the interpretation of infant reflex behavior has changed in recent years (Tronick & Adamson, 1980). At one time researchers considered infant behavior to be regulated entirely by reflexes, as if the infant were pre-wired. This implied that only the more primitive parts of the nervous system could account for infant behavior. There is growing evidence that the infant uses the whole brain. The behavior that appears to be "wired in" provides preparation for dealing with the environment. The reflex behaviors seen in newborns provide the foundation for later development and permit the infant to respond to stimuli (Tronick & Adamson, 1980). Primitive reflexes contribute to survival and establish the basis for voluntary control. The importance of reflexive behavior is its relevance to later voluntary movement (Brazelton, 1977).

Two types of reflex systems are present in the infant. Reflexes of the first type make their appearance at birth; these are the primitive reflexes (see Figure 2.1). When voluntary control has been established, these reflexes disappear. Persistence of primitive reflexes is associated with damage to the infant nervous system that is likely to interfere with normal development. For example, the potential for exploratory behavior is reduced in infants with a persistent tonic neck reflex. Persistence of primitive reflexes prevents the onset of voluntary, and thus controlled, actions of the head, arms and legs (Garwood, 1983).

The second type of reflex system is represented by automatic reflexes, the "righting" and equilibrium reactions. Automatic reflexes regulate posture and are the basis of balance and equilibrium. Righting reactions restore normal posture and permit the infant to maintain the position of the head in alignment with the rest of the body (Connor, Williamson, & Siepp, 1978). "Righting" allows for rotation of the body. Equilibrium reactions are balance responses; they incorporate righting reflexes and permit the maintainance of balance in a variety of postures. Automatic reflexes are not present at birth.

Primitive reflexes prepare infants for acts of standing and walking and use of arms and hands (Tronick & Adamson, 1980). Primitive reflexes are inhibited as righting and equilibrium reactions allow for ever-increasing voluntary movement. When reflexive movement patterns

FIGURE 2.1. Primitive Reflexes

Assymetrical Tonic Neck. This reflex is observed when the infant's head is turned to one side and the arm on the opposite side straightens. This reflex has usually disappeared by the time the infant is six months of age.

Grasp. This reflex appears when pressure is applied to the palm of the hand, causing the fingers to close automatically around the object. This reflex disappears when the infant can voluntarily grasp objects at about five or six months of age.

Moro. This reflex is an outward thrusting of the arms when there is backward extension of the head. Absence of the Moro reflex at birth or its persistence after six months of age usually indicates neurological dysfunction.

Rooting. This reflex is caused by pressure on the infant's cheek; the head turns and the mouth opens as if the infant were searching for the source of food.

Sucking. This reflex appears when the infant's lips or gums are lightly touched. This reflex disappears at about three months.

Tonic Labyrinthine. This reflex depends on the position of the head. In a prone position, the infant's arms and legs are bent under his body and head and neck are flexed. If infants are lying on their backs, their posture is characterized by straight legs, retracted shoulders, arched neck, and head pressed against the surface beneath.

---

continue to dominate, the consequence is poor movement patterns and delay of motor development.

Abnormal muscle tone (hyper- or hypotonia) is associated with the persistence of primitive reflexes. Too little tone, or hypotonia, leads to difficulty with head control, slowed responses to sensory stimuli, problems with weight bearing, and delay in ability to hold the spine erect (Connor, Williamson, & Siepp, 1978). Too much tone, or hypertonia, makes smooth movement difficult. Children with hypertonia tend to overreact to stimuli and to be limited in their range of motion. A condition of abnormal fluctuation of tone (or dystonia) also makes controlled movement difficult and delays the onset of the reciprocal movement patterns basic to creeping and walking.

Recovery from Brain Damage

Damage to the nervous system in infancy has variable consequences. As noted in the previous chapter, the human nervous system has considerable reserves; its capacity to heal itself and overcome the effects of early trauma are dependent on a number of factors. In general, recovery of many types of brain insult are more complete in infancy than if the same insult were to occur in adulthood. The size and nature of the insult are determining factors in the recovery of function. Environmental influences and genetic endowment also act to modify cerebral dysfunction after injury (Towbin, 1981). Brain damage sustained during the perinatal period (three months before and after birth) commonly includes motor disabilities, epilepsy, and associated difficulties of sensorimotor integration (Towbin, 1981). Damage to the delicate infant nervous system interferes with stable control over such physiological states as, for example, maintaining wakefulness and alertness. Additional consequences of nervous system damage may delay or prevent the onset of speech and affect other aspects of learning.

Severe forms of social and sensory deprivation also have damaging effects on the onset of speech. Studies of children raised in deprived and depriving environments demonstrate the effects of social deprivation. The story of Victor, faithfully recorded by Itard (1806/1972), portrays the severe effects of social deprivation. Victor was eleven years of age when he was discovered in the woods of Caune, France. Itard, a young physician, brought Victor into his home in order to educate him. Itard was impressed by Victor's uneven and highly selective responses to sensory stimuli. For example, Victor could hear a walnut being cracked, but he seemed not to hear the sound of rifle shots. Itard wrote:

> His [Victor's] eyes were without steadiness, without expression, wandering from one object to another, without fixing on anything; so little instructed in other respects, and so little experienced in the sense of touch, that he was unable to distinguish between an object in relief and a painting: the organ of hearing was alike insensible to the loudest noises and to the most charming music. (Itard, 1806/1972, p. 97)

The nervous system is made inefficient by injury or maldevelopment; its efficiency is marred by under- or overresponding to sensory stimuli. Environments that regulate sensory input and tailor stimulation to the needs of handicapped infants improve the efficiency of the system. Nevertheless, the normal accomplishments of the first years of life take longer to establish.

Learning In Infancy

Development is characterized by the emergence of increasingly complex levels of mental organization. With control over states of alertness comes readiness to interact with the environment. Voluntary behavior replaces the reflex actions of the newborn. As infants interact with their environments, they gain the skills to explore and manipulate objects and communicate with their worlds.

The first year is typically one of rapid growth. Birth weights triple and height increases by five or six inches. Infants experience an infinite number of sensations. Sights, sounds, smells, tastes, and kinesthetic and tactile sensations become linked to one another in multiple and meaningful ways. Thousands of encounters with their social and physical worlds enable the integration of sensory experiences. Sounds are associated with sights, tastes with smells, touch with action. Infants internalize their actions and the sensations that result from them.

Learning, according to Piaget (1958), takes place in active encounter with the environment. Active encounters or interactions enable the formation of ideas or notions about people and objects. Piaget (1958) called these ideas "action schemata." The action schema represents both the actions performed on objects and the sensations created by the actions. For example, holding a rattle and seeing it or shaking the rattle and hearing it become fused into one experience. The sensory and motor elements of every action are fused and experienced as a single unit. These sensorimotor units are practiced over and over again until they are internalized and become a specific schema in the mind. Thus, every experience has two distinct elements: muscular action and sensory feedback (Stern, 1977). The more experiences infants have, the more they learn.

During the interaction of infants and adults, there are many sensory events that co-occur, or happen simultaneously (Bricker & Lewis, 1982). Co-occurrences enhance sensory experiences and focus infant attention, thereby facilitating responsiveness. Bricker and Lewis noted that whatever the co-occurrence, "the basic adaptive structure is to detect, to associate, and to remember such co-occurrences" (1982, p. 2). Interactions within the environment are thus seen as the source of information gathering.

The first stage of development, which Piaget called the "sensorimotor period," is characterized by the appearance of perceptual, motor, and language capacities. Thousands of active encounters with people, objects, and events are the basis of sensorimotor knowledge. Williams (1982) pointed out that realistic notions of objects and events are based on clear perceptions of objects and events.

During the sensorimotor period the skills and behavior needed to organize and adapt to the environment are established. Mastery skills (such as the handling and manipulating of objects), awareness of self and others, and language and other forms of symbolic behavior are all established. It is not possible to disentangle the strands of social and cognitive development in infancy or early childhood.

The Social Competence of Infants

The social competence of infants resides in their capacities to gain and maintain adults' attention and mutuality of responsiveness. Infants are social beings, and their earliest encounters are both transactional and reciprocal. The earliest social encounters establish the intimate attachments between mother and child. So begins the unfolding of the human personality. Infants' awareness of adults as separate from themselves motivates them to communicate and establish strategies for nonverbal conversation (Wolff, 1981). Social interchanges between infants and adults instruct infants in the techniques of reciprocal interaction, such as sharing knowledge and turn-taking (Wolff, 1981).

Mothers teach their infants about reciprocal relationships when they play social games like "peek-a-boo" with them. These social games or routines have well-marked beginnings and endings, which give them pattern and regularity. Routines such as "peek-a-boo" include a climax, such as a sound or a tickle (Bruner & Sherwood, 1976). The vocal expressions that are part of these social games are clearly preadaptive to later acquisition of language forms (McLean & Snyder-McLean, 1978). Infants and their mothers share attention to the sequence of events of social routines; in this manner mothers show their infants how to share attention and take turns responding.

Infant Communication

Visual contact or gaze behaviors play a central role in the establishment of communication in infancy. Gaze behaviors describe infants' visual regard of their mothers' faces. These behaviors are well organized in early infancy. By four months of age infants are able to use gaze behavior to initiate, maintain, terminate, or avoid interactions (Stern, 1977). Mutual visual regard is a highly visible and arousing stimulus. Other developing abilities also come into play. Increased head control enables the turning of the head and body to achieve face-to-face contact. Increased control of the arms and hands comes with attainment of the sitting posture. By five or six months of age, normal infants use head and body postures as well as gaze to signal readiness for interaction (Stern, 1977). Adults respond to their infants' body signals with communicating behaviors of their own.

Tronick and his colleagues (Tronick & Adamson, 1980) investigated the behavior of infants when their mothers were asked to perform in unusual or unexpected ways. Mothers were requested to interact with their infants in normal fashion and then to remain still-faced for three minutes. The reactions of the infants to their still-faced mothers was dramatic. When the mothers failed to respond to the greetings of their infants, the infants became still, stared, turned away, and then tried again to elicit a response. Again, when still no response was forthcoming, the infants gazed at their mothers warily and turned away. Continuation of nonresponsiveness by the mothers produced still more wary behavior; infants turned their gazes, faces, and bodies away from their mothers. When the period of the mothers' nonresponsiveness was extended, the infants reacted with anxiety and crying. Some of the infants in this experiment lost postural self-control; others engaged in self-comforting behaviors.

Changes in mothers' behavior produce modifications in their infants' responses to them. Infants reach out and make calling vocalizations when their mothers do not look directly at them (Tronick & Adamson, 1980). When Tronick and his co-workers asked the mothers to act like puppets and jerk their heads and arms, the infants stared at their mothers as if in disbelief (Tronick & Adamson, 1980). Infants display greater responsiveness when mothers slow down the pace of their interactions.

Infant studies suggest that difficulties may arise when mothers perform their actions too quickly. When infants are unable to follow their mothers' actions, they look away (Tronick, 1981). Mothers who by nature perform too quickly do not give their infants a chance to respond. Infants need time to organize their own responses.

Als, Tronick, and Brazelton (1980) studied the interactions of a blind infant and her sighted mother and demonstrated how mutuality of response can be achieved: the infant, recognizing her mother's touch and voice, responded with increased touching. Touch combined with voice became the mode of interaction between infant and mother; the infant learned to use auditory and tactile stimulation to control her own interactive behaviors.

A study of a sighted infant with blind parents revealed similar findings. The sighted infant used touch and voice to contact her parents, not gaze. She looked off to the side while cooing and moving with her parents' playful talk, songs, and touches. With sighted adults, the same infant used gaze behaviors.

Outcomes of Interaction

Independent activity, imitation, and adaptability to the changing demands of the social environment are outcomes of social interaction.

At first, play with mothers and play with objects are separate activities. Sometime between 9 and 13 months, infants begin to incorporate objects into their social games (Tronick & Adamson, 1980). Six-month-old infants either interact socially or exercise their object skills.

Tronick and Adamson (1980) theorize that infants learn to regulate their mothers' attention before they can direct their mothers' attention to an external event. Reference to the parent comes before reference to objects or other external events. Adults play a significant role by calling infants' attention to objects and their uses. Infants learn how to play with objects from watching their mothers' play.

Independent activity is another outcome of social interaction. Children learn to do things independently and follow the requests of adults. Wertsch (1979) hypothesized that independent action is acquired in a sequence. For example, the adult makes a request for the child to do something and then guides the child in doing it, such as a mother telling her child to wash and helping with actions of face washing. Thus the task is stated and the child guided in its performance. As proficiency is gained, the adult only needs to state the task and the child performs independently. Other outcomes of interaction include the achievements that characterize learning during the sensorimotor period:

Communication skills, including language
Goal-directed behaviors, such as exploration and manipulation of
    objects
Realistic interpretations of sensory information, object recognition
Concepts of self, space, time, and causality
Symbolic behavior, including language and symbolic play

The social interaction of infants with their adult partners provides the social context for these accomplishments. Social interaction is a source of learning. During the course of interactions with their parents, infants learn a variety of concepts and skills; most importantly they are learning about people and how they behave toward one another. The ability of infants to interact with their environments is the fundamental adaptive act of infancy (Bricker & Lewis, 1982).

Research Studies on Developmentally Delayed Infants

The research on handicapped infants highlights the importance of environmental and social interaction. Rowland (1984) found a substantial delay among the blind infants in her study and concluded that the poorly developed vocal patterns of the infants may reflect a lack of consistent vocal input and weak responses to infants' vocalizations from their mothers. Rowland reasoned that since speech, rather than gestures, will probably be the first referential behavior produced by blind children, a tightly structured program of parental vocalizations and responses to infants' vocalizations should be beneficial.

Maternal responsiveness has been correlated with infant IQ scores as measured by the Bayley Mental Development Index. Coates and Lewis (cited in Bricker & Lewis, 1982) investigated two types of maternal responsiveness: proximal (touching and holding) and distal (looking at, smiling, or vocalizing). Coates and Lewis concluded that the younger the infants, the more dependent they are on proximal responses. Proximal responses were related to the scores on the Mental Development Index.

Babies with limited response repertoires have an inhibiting effect on their parents (Bricker & Lewis, 1982). The inability of parents to achieve successful contact with their infants effectively limits the number of co-occurrences encountered by their infants. The more handicapped infants have fewer resources available through which to initiate interaction. Unresponsive infants elicit fewer responses from adults.

The drive toward mastery and object knowledge is hampered by difficulties of physical control. Visual impairments combined with failure to control head and hand delay and repress the drive toward mastery. Conditions causing too much or too little muscle tone in the arms and hands (hypertonia and hypotonia, respectively) may delay or completely prevent the manipulation of objects. Vietze and his co-workers (1983) found that infants with Down's syndrome (who tend to be hypotonic) spend more time looking at toys and other objects than handling them. Their mothers reported that their infants showed little interest in handling or exploring the toys.

Social interaction is disrupted by lack of eye contact and other signal-type behaviors that guide mothers in "play" with their infants. (Field, 1983). Visual gaze, head movements, and facial expressions are most easily read by parents as signals. A fundamental issue in the intervention of visually impaired developmentally delayed infants is the establishment of interaction with both the social and physical environments. Parents who are having difficulty in establishing intimacy with their infants are unable to establish contingency between their own actions and the actions of their infants (Kalveboer, 1979).

Research data suggest that developmentally delayed infants require more deliberate efforts on the part of parents to be responsive. The consequences of too little interaction are devastating; they prevent the establishment of links between infants and their environments. Lack of relatedness, spontaneity, and curiosity are characteristics of social isolation, not handicapping conditions.

Implications for Intervention

It is tragically easy for the most caring parents to lose essential intimacy with their handicapped infants. Alone or in combination, a number of factors—grief, guilt, fear, or simply not knowing how to handle their babies—can lead to a social distancing that make it impossible for parent and child to enjoy mutual responsiveness. Until the social distance is bridged and closeness is established, visually impaired infants, even when no other diagnosable condition is present, are unable to establish vital links with their environments. Mothers of handicapped infants may need to be shown how to encourage the cycle of mutually satisfying responsiveness of social interaction (Als, Tronick & Brazelton, 1980). Increasing mothers' responsivity to infants in the absence of guidance from their infants is an important goal of intervention in infancy.

Increased responsivity helps to focus infants' attention on co-occurrences of sensory events. More repetition and heightened sensation are ways of increasing responsivity and helping infants to negotiate their interactions. For example, simultaneously holding or touching while talking, cooing, or singing provides the infant with multiple sensory experience. Intensified co-occurrences help to establish "the vital connection" between infants and their mothers. Infants' awareness of their mothers is encouraged with heightened sensory input, such as simultaneous vocalization, hand holding, containment, and other bodily actions. Infants' awareness of their mothers' actions leads to anticipation and responsivity. The ways in which infants respond to their mothers should be treated as communicative behavior. As Als, Tronick, and Brazelton (1980) suggested, when mothers treat the actions of their infants as communicative, they help their infants to interact.

As mothers become aware of the meanings of their visually impaired infants' behaviors, they begin to select from the infant's own repertoire. Knowing how to use her baby's hands to achieve contact, a mother might take her infant's hand and bring it to her face, thus showing the infant how to make contact with her. As mothers become proficient at reinforcing their infants' behaviors, they increase both their own and their babies' interactive repertoires. Their responses to their infants provide necessary feedback.

Rowland (1984) suggested that reciprocal responding between blind infants and their mothers could be reinforced by giving infants cues. A mother's placing her mouth on her infant's cheek or hand as she speaks alerts her child to the act of speech. Rowland emphasized that parents should speak in short bursts alternated with short periods of silence. The silence cues the infants' turn for speaking (vocalizing). As Rowland noted, the failure to establish mutually satisfying communicative interactions during these early months is difficult to remedy.

Handicapped infants may be able to sustain only brief and fleeting attention, but persistence is eventually rewarded with increased attention and longer periods of interaction. Working within the limits of the infant's attention span helps interaction to develop comfortably. Some blind babies resist being held, and other ways need to be found to achieve intimacy. Even with sensitive babies, holding, if only for brief periods, should be encouraged. Parents may need to experiment with different ways of holding their infants. One mother of a resistant infant placed her infant on her bed and lay next to her while she was feeding, gently talking to, and stroking her. It was not long before this infant permitted holding.

Intervention services designed to provide parents with the skills to establish interactions with their infants encourage intimacy and deeply enrich the relationships between parents and their children.

Issues in Early Intervention

The purpose of early intervention is to insure a good beginning for handicapped infants and their parents. Early intervention is as much concerned with the family as with the child. Service plans for families include access to information as well as practical assistance. Medical and social services, parent education and counseling, respite care, and baby-sitting services are all part of a comprehensive service plan. Referral to appropriate service agencies is important, but a stronger need may be getting to know other families who are coping with handicapped infants (Fewell, 1983).

Not all families require the same services. Families differ in their response to the birth of a handicapped child. Some conditions are not identified at birth and many months may pass before the child is identified as having problems. Some parents simply need encouragement and practical advice, while others may need counseling and ongoing support.

A mother of a multihandicapped five-month-old baby was attending a conference on blind infants and young children. She attended every session and took many notes. Her baby had been born prematurely and was kept in the hospital nursery for two months. When she was finally able to bring her baby home, she felt at a loss.

"I stand by her crib and feel so helpless. I don't know how to treat her. She is so tiny and she doesn't seem to respond to me at all," the young mother told one of the speakers at the conference. The speaker noted the tension in the mother's face and gently asked several questions, learning that several people came to her home to help—a social worker, a physical therapist, and an infant development worker. The baby was receiving therapy several times a week, but no one had shown the mother how to handle her infant, or even encouraged her to hold her.

Not knowing what to advise the mother, the speaker simply asked, "Can you play with your baby, hold her and sing to her?"

"You mean that it would be all right just to play with her?" the young mother said, relief flooding her face. "That's exactly what I want to be able to do."

In the absence of knowing what to expect, parents feel bewildered and have little confidence in their parenting abilities. This incident illustrates the value of putting inexperienced mothers in touch with experienced mothers of handicapped babies.

Assessment of Infants

The major purpose of assessment is the identification of abilities. Assessment profiles should lead to a set of detailed program objectives, reflecting the needs of infants and their families. Assessment procedures designed for sighted infants have little application to visually impaired infants. Active use of the senses of touch and hearing are the modes of interaction available to blind babies. Infants with developmental problems in addition to visual impairments can be expected to take longer to achieve developmental milestones. As Hammer (1984) noted, they have a longer "growing season" and require carefully planned experiences and opportunities for learning.

Assessment of these infants is ongoing and cannot be separated from education and treatment. Motivational and environmental considerations need to be assessed along with motor, social, and communicative behavior. Assessment of the infant should be part of the comprehensive service plan. Considerations in the assessment process should include medical information regarding the cause of disability, visual and auditory acuity, gross and fine motor development, and social behavior. Family characteristics, such as the number of adults in the home, number of siblings, and the need of the mother to work outside of the home, are also important considerations. Availability of services and parents' perceptions of what they require contribute to the making of a comprehensive intervention plan. Fewell (1983) placed health needs first on the list of areas to be assessed. Other areas include:

Vision: It is often very difficult to accurately assess the visual potential of infants. As much information as can be gathered about the cause of the visual impairment is extremely helpful. Children who have no diagnosable visual problem should not be assumed to have no sight, even in the absence of clearly defined looking behaviors.

Hearing: This may also be difficult to assess, especially in the absence of vision. Because even mild hearing impairments in combination with visual handicaps represent severe sensory loss, hearing should be carefully investigated. While Hart (1984) acknowledges the difficulties of obtaining accurate auditory assessments in infancy, she suggests that ongoing informal assessments yield valuable information.

Movement: It is important to know how much and what kinds of movement the child can perform independently. Mobility is related to motivation as well as to neuromotor function. Normal movement can be facilitated through proper handling, positioning, carrying, and so forth. The importance of muscle tone in relation to movement cannot be overemphasized. Muscle tone indicates the degree of tension in body musculature. Too much or too little tone affects the control of body movement and body posture. Neurodevelopmental therapy emphasizes movement to build up normal tone and reduce abnormal tone, and encourages employing the prone position to develop head balance and the musculature of the shoulders and arms (Hart, 1984). Problems in feeding may indicate disorders of the musculature of the head, neck, mouth, and throat that can delay the onset of speech (Fewell, 1983).

Vocal behavior: The range and amount of nonspeech vocalization indicate the abilities to control the musculature of the lips and tongue. The association of vocal behavior with social interaction is an important index of the potential for speech.

Manual ability: Infants' abilities to use their hands for grasping, holding, banging, or otherwise handling objects reveal their interest and their potential for a wide assortment of mastery skills. Lack of control of the hand tends to prevent exploration and manipulation of objects.

Social responsiveness: The enjoyment indicated by interacting with other people reveals the child's state of emotional well-being. It is important to know if there is recognition of familiar people, initiation of interaction, or avoidance of social contact (Fewell, 1983).

Transdisciplinary Teams

The transdisciplinary approach recognizes the critical role of parents in caring for their own infants. The role of professionals is to pool and coordinate their individual expertise in order to guide parents or other caregivers. One member of the transdisciplinary team assumes the responsibility of helping the family interpret the information and decide on a treatment plan. This approach combines acknowledgment that parents are the child's first teachers with the value of the multidisciplinary team (Connor, Williamson, & Siepp, 1978).

In traditional multiprofessional teams, assessments are completed by different types of professionals, such as physicians, educators, psychologists, speech pathologists, physical and occupational therapists, and infant development workers. The results are collected and presented to the parents, often without opportunity for informal discussion or questioning by parents. Sometimes the opinions of the different team members seem to be worlds apart and parents are given contradictory or fragmented advice.

Transdisciplinary approaches attempt to overcome these communication problems. As they blur the edges of individual professional roles, they change the focus from the professional to the parent, and reduce the number of professionals to whom the infant must adapt. Working directly with parents has proven to be enormously effective. By providing parents with the expertise they need, continuity and consistency are more easily achieved.

Models of Infant Intervention

In general there are two types of intervention programs. One type is based in the infant's home and the other requires that the infant be brought to a center. Each has advantages. Home-based intervention makes it possible to include other family members and does not disrupt the infant's or the family's routines (Bronfenbrenner, 1975). Home-based programs focus on helping the caregivers become effective interveners.

Center-based models, on the other hand, offer parents opportunities to meet with other parents and observe other children. For the youngest children, especially those with ongoing medical problems, home-based programs are indicated. Bronfenbrenner (1975) identified the following characteristics of effective intervention programs.

The program philosophy is clearly stated; its goals and purposes are well defined.

The criteria by which progress is to be measured in each developmental domain are well defined and specific; the behaviors the infant is expected to develop and the activities and procedures designed to develop the behavior are clearly identified.

The program is staffed by qualified and appropriately trained individuals.

The families of the infants are involved in the planning and execution of the program.

The program includes a method of evaluation of infants' progress.

Summary

The primary aim of early intervention programs is to help parents develop the means and resources of nurturing their own babies. Practical support to the family is the highest priority during infancy and early childhood. Extended periods of hospitalization, prematurity, and related medical treatments may delay the formation of emotional bonding and the parent/infant partnership that is essential to healthy emotional development. Parents who are confident, relaxed, and secure in their knowledge of how to encourage responsiveness are able to establish close intimate relationships with their handicapped infants. Professional teams can offer strong support and guidance to parents and other caregivers by providing coordinated, cohesive, and practical guidance in such matters as needed alterations to the physical environment, sensory stimulation, and the skills to coax and encourage social responsiveness.

3.

Visual Impairments and Associated Neurological and Developmental Handicaps

Educating visually impaired children demands an understanding of how handicapping conditions disguise, delay, disrupt, or prevent expressions of mental ability. The purpose of this chapter is to explore the nature of visually handicapping conditions, associated developmental disabilities, and their effects on development and learning.

Impairment, whether visual, physical, or mental, implies deficit and disability. But there is much more than that. If the impairment is the focus of attention, rather than the child, there is the risk of losing sight of the child behind the label. On the other hand, if the handicaps are not understood in relation to developmental tasks, there is the risk of not appreciating the obstacles that must be overcome on the path to optimal development. In different ways and in different degrees, visual, physical, or mental impairments interfere with gaining mastery of developmental tasks. It is important to appreciate the mechanisms of interference in order to plan strategies of intervention.

Visual Impairments

Age of onset of visual impairments is an important consideration, particularly as it distinguishes those individuals who were born with visual impairments from those who acquired their condition after the age of three or four years. *Congenital* visual impairments are present at birth. *Adventitious* blindness refers to handicaps that are acquired some time after birth. The psychological implications of this distinction increase with the age of the individual. Older children and adults who have grown up with full use of their vision face major psychological adjustment to the loss of sight (Barraga, 1976).

Visual impairments are also classified according to the degree of visual loss as defined by measures of visual acuity. The term *legal blindness,* for example, is used to determine eligibility for social and education services. Terms that define "legal" blindness vary from country to country; there are some 65 different definitions of blindness used around the world (Colenbrander, 1976). In North America and most of western Europe, persons are considered entitled to services if they have a measured visual acuity of 20/200 (6/60) or less in the better eye with the best correction; or if the widest diameter of the field of vision is an angle no greater than 20 degrees. Acuity measures of 20/70 to 20/200 define the population of the partially sighted.

Barraga (1976) described visually impaired children as those who have visual disabilities that interfere with their ability to learn and who require adaptations in "teaching methods, learning materials and/or of the learning environment" (p. 16). Because the developmental and educational consequences of impaired vision are severe, the trend toward functional classifications of visual impairments is an important one. Functional classifications indicate the nature of the assistance required. Faye (1976a) classified persons with visual impairments according to their functional vision. Faye's five categories range from persons with mild impairments to those who are totally blind. The first group consists of those who have near-normal vision but who require corrective lenses and reading aids. The second group has a moderate reduction in visual acuity and may require special lighting and visual aids, but has no significant field losses. The third group has reduced central vision, moderate field losses, and may experience inability to cope physically or psychologically with their impaired vision. This group includes people who qualify for specialized services for the visually impaired. The fourth group has poor functional vision, marked field losses, or poor central vision, and requires strong reading aids. The fifth group consists of people who are totally blind.

Visual impairments may change over time, and some children experience fluctuations in their vision. It is important to recognize that two children can have the same type and degree of visual impairment and yet adjust in very different ways. Psychological and emotional factors profoundly influence the way the children cope with visual impairments (Barraga, 1976). Throughout this book, the terms *visually impaired* or *low vision* will be used to describe children who have some degree of vision; the term *blindness* will be used only to describe children who have no sight.

The Visual Process

It is useful to review the visual process in order to appreciate the scope of disability caused by the absence of sight, or reduced visual abilities. The eye is composed of three tissue layers: The outer layer is composed of the sclera and cornea; the middle layer contains the iris, lens, and the optical muscles; the inner layer contains the retina (see Figure 3.1). Strong connective tissues and skeletal bone surround, support, and protect the eye.

Visual activity begins in the light-sensitive nerve cells of the retina. Chemical changes produced by light energy in photosensitive cells give rise to electrical activity that is communicated to cortical and sub-cortical levels of the brain (Haith, 1980). Light enters the eye from the surface of the cornea and then penetrates through the anterior chamber, the crystalline lens, and posterior chamber to the photosensitive nerve cells embedded in the retina. Visual impairments are associated with interference with or blocking of:

The passage of light through the eye
The focusing of light on the retina
The transmission of light images to the brain via the retina and
  optic nerve
The brain's ability to receive and interpret visual images

The following terms are important to understanding the workings of the visual system.

Visual acuity: A physical measurement of the ability of the eye to see details of objects or symbols at specified distances. Acuity can be measured for both near and far objects. The first number in an acuity measure is the distance at which vision is measured, which is usually 20 feet (or 6 meters). The second number refers to the size of image that can be seen at that distance. For example, normal vision is represented as 20/20, meaning that from a distance of 20 feet, the normal eye can see letters, numbers, or symbols of a size standardized for that distance on a chart. (The Snellen chart is the most commonly used.) An individual with an acuity measure of 20/70 may have adequate vision for gross object perception, but not for seeing fine details at a distance of 6 feet (Faye, 1976a). Acuity measures vary with lighting conditions, familiarity, maturity, fatigue, the effect of movement, and other factors. Assessments of visual acuity taken in test situations may be measures of maximum achieved acuity under optimum conditions and may differ from the way the child functions in school. Acuity measures do not predict how well children utilize their remaining vision (Barraga, 1976; Faye, 1976a).

FIGURE 3.1. Important Structures of the Eye

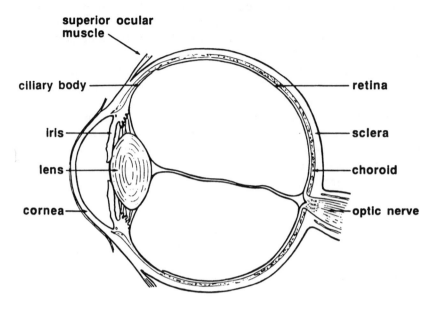

Cornea. This transparent membrane covers the front of the eye. The cornea is the first of the light transmitting structures and must be clear and free of any blemish. It is continuous with the **sclera**, commonly recognized as the white of the eye.

Lens. The crystalline lens can change its focusing power, enabling the eye to focus on near or distant objects. The shape of the lens is controlled by a muscle in the **ciliary body**.

Iris. The iris gives the eye its color and regulates the size of the pupil in response to the intensity of light.

Retina. Light sensitive nerve cells, the rods and cones, are embedded in the retina, the innermost layer of the eye. The cone cells, which are concentrated in the central area of the retina, enable color vision; rod cells, which predominate in the rest of the retina, respond to the brightness of light and are more sensitive to low light levels. Blood is supplied to the retina by the choroid, the tissue layer beneath the sclera.

Ocular muscles. Three pairs of ocular muscles control and synchronize the movements of the eyes. Perfect synchronization between the two eyes is necessary for depth perception (Harley & Lawrence, 1977).

Visual fields: Measures of visual fields concern the angle of view. There are two categories of visual field: central and peripheral. Some children have good central fields and severely limited peripheral fields; others have better peripheral than central vision. If the field of vision is less than 10 degrees, the child will not be able to read comfortably (J. Jantzi, personal communication, 1985). This condition causes the individual to experience vision as if looking at the world through two narrow tubes.

Visual efficiency: This describes how well an individual is able to utilize residual vision. Fluctuations of sight caused by sensitivity to light, degenerative conditions, and interference in the visual field must be considered in the assessment of visual efficiency. It is important for parents and teachers to know how students use their remaining vision. There are aspects of vision that are dependent on motivation and experience (Barraga, 1976).

Classification of Visual Impairments

Severe visual handicaps frequently combine more than one visual impairment. However, for purposes of clarity, visual impairments will be discussed in the following categories:

Refractive disorders
Oculomotor disorders
Pathologies and malformations of the eye
Perceptual disorders

Refractive Disorders.   Refraction refers to the bending of light. As light passes through the refractive structures of the normal eye, particularly the cornea and lens, it is bent so that rays of light fall on the most light-sensitive portion of the retina. This central portion of the retina is called the *fovea.* Refractive errors occur when the light image is not perfectly focused on the retina. In the vast majority of cases, prescription lenses are capable of correcting most refractive faults. There are four types of refractive errors:

Myopia (nearsightedness): This is the single greatest cause of defective vision in children (Harley & Lawrence, 1977). Lens or cornea defects or elongation of the eyeball cause light rays to be brought into focus in front of the retina instead of on it. As a result, focus gets worse as distance from the eye increases. Severe forms of myopia are often associated with eye disease and other visual disorders (Curtin, 1976).

Hyperopia (farsightedness): This condition is often thought of as the opposite of myopia because it entails light rays being brought into focus behind the retina. It may result from an eye that is too small. Uncorrected hyperopia interferes with near vision (Faye, 1976A).

Astigmatism: Irregularity in the normally smooth surface of the cornea that causes light rays to be refracted in a random fashion that interferes with clarity of vision. Astigmatism results from an uneven curvature of the cornea. Significant degrees of astigmatism interfere with both distance vision and reading (Faye, 1976a).

Presbyopia: The loss of focusing power of the lens that affects most people after the age of 40. The lens loses some of its accommodative capacity, and the individual is no longer able to read small print without prescription lenses.

Refractive disorders sometimes occur in association with oculomotor problems or eye disease. In these instances, corrective lenses may improve sight but will not restore full vision.

Oculomotor Problems. In normal vision, the images from each eye are fused in the visual centers of the brain so that only one image is perceived. If the brain receives two disparate images from the eyes, it suppresses the image from one, resulting in blindness in that eye. The musculature of the eyes is synchronized so that the images can be fused. Oculomotor problems occur when one or both eyes cannot control gaze, a condition that results in seriously impaired vision. There are two primary types of oculomotor problems:

Strabismus: Weakness in the musculature of the eye, causing the eyes to converge (cross) or diverge. Strabismus may occur in one or both eyes. It may be intermittent, appearing only when the eye is fatigued, or it may be constant.

Nystagmus: This is a condition in which the natural movements of the eye are grossly exaggerated, resulting in uncontrolled eye movements. This condition is often found in association with neurological impairments and seriously affects perceptual efficiency (Van der Heyden, 1979). When nystagmus is present, it is likely to be associated with seriously defective vision (Faye, 1976a). Children instinctively adopt those head postures that reduce nystagmus to a minimum.

Pathologies and Malformations of the Eye. The following pathological conditions are the most common causes of blindness and severe visual impairment in children:

Cataracts: A progressive clouding of the crystalline lens that restricts the ability of the eye to receive light. Cataracts may be associated with injury, infection, metabolic disorders, or toxic conditions

(Harley & Lawrence, 1977). Bilateral cataracts in children are often associated with nystagmus and retinal disease (Van Dijk, 1982).

Glaucoma: A structural problem causing blockage of the fluid that normally circulates within the eye. The resulting increase in intraocular pressure can damage the optic nerve and cause the eye to become misshapen (Harley & Lawrence, 1977). Glaucoma can occur at birth or develop later in childhood or adulthood. Congenital glaucoma may exist by itself or in association with other pathological conditions.

Optic atrophy: Complete or partial destruction of the optic nerve that causes the damaged nerve fibers of the optic disk to atrophy. Optic atrophy can be congenital or acquired in later life. It may also be the result of injury, such as a blow to the eye. The condition can exist by itself or in association with other eye disorders (Harley & Lawrence, 1977).

Retinitis pigmentosa: An inherited disease causing retinal tissue to degenerate. Both the severity of the condition and age of onset vary with the individual (Harley & Lawrence, 1977). Age of onset ranges from childhood to early adulthood. Usher's syndrome, a condition in which retinitis pigmentosa occurs in combination with familial nerve deafness, is a major cause of deaf/blindness among children. Cataracts or glaucoma sometimes accompany retinitis pigmentosa.

Retrolental fibroplasia (RLF): A severe impairment caused by oxygen during the incubation of premature infants (Harley & Lawrence, 1977). The condition is sometimes referred to as retinopathy of infancy. RLF has been successfully prevented with close monitoring of the amount of oxygen given to incubated infants. However, RLF has not been eliminated and tends to affect infants weighing less than two kilograms (four and a half pounds) at birth.

Macular retinal degeneration: The destruction or poor development of the macular (central) portion of the retina. Often undetected in young children, its consequence is extremely poor central vision. This condition may be inherited or caused by injuries to the eye (Harley & Lawrence, 1977).

Diabetic retinopathy: A major cause of blindness in young adults with diabetes. Blindness is caused by damage to the blood vessels of the eye, especially in the retina (Harley & Lawrence, 1977).

Albinism: Lack of pigment in all parts of the body; the skin is white and the hair is pale yellow in both Caucasians and non-Caucasians. Albinism often entails photophobia (acute sensitivity to light) and may be accompanied by astigmatism and nystagmus.

There is a severe loss of visual acuity in children with albinism (Harley & Lawrence, 1977).

Retinal detachment: A separation of the outer layer of the retina from other retinal tissue. It can be caused by a sharp blow to the head. Laser beam surgery has been successful in reattaching the retina where there has been only partial damage.

Malformations of the eye: Conditions in which the eye has failed to form fully are divided into two types. *Anophlamia* describes the complete absence or partial development of the eyeball. In *microphthalmia* the eye is small and may be misshapen. Microphthalmia is often associated with other conditions. Structural anomalies may be associated with ocular diseases such as glaucoma.

Visual Perceptual Disorders.   Visual perceptual disorders are included here because of their frequent association with neurological disorders and/or conditions of visual deprivation associated with severely impaired vision. From an educational point of view, visual perceptual problems are important to visual efficiency.

Visual perceptual disorders may be associated with malfunctions and lesions in the nerve pathways serving the visual system. Damage to the nerve pathways can interfere with the transmission of visual images by distorting them or preventing them from reaching the visual cortex of the brain. Perceptual disorders may explain the poor utilization of visual images in sighted children with other developmental disabilities.

Perceptual deficits or disabilities are reflected behaviorally in a variety of performance deficits. These include failure to recognize faces, objects, or pictorial representations; difficulties in making judgments about distance and location; and/or inability to draw or write (Benton, 1979b). Much of what is understood about perceptual disorders comes from clinical studies of adult stroke patients. Children with neurological impairments have problems that may be strikingly similar to adult stroke patients.

The term *cortical blindness* generally implies that there has been damage to the visual cortex. A lesion or abnormality of the visual cortex may hinder or prevent visual nerve impulses from reaching the brain and/or make it difficult for the brain to interpret visual information. The nature of the damage determines the type and extent of loss. Three main types of visual perceptual disorders have been defined by Benton (1979b, p. 189) as:

Visuoperceptual disorders: Inability to recognize faces or objects

Visuospatial disorders: Defective judgment of spatial relationships and difficulty in localizing objects. A child with this type of perceptual disorder is unable to reach for objects with accuracy and may neglect visual stimuli on one side of his or her body.

Visuoconstructive disorders: Inability to write or draw or complete assembly tasks

These problems are deeply disturbing and affect the efficiency of psychological function.

Developmental Consequences of Visual Impairments

Severe visual impairments impose many restrictions on the ease of social and environmental interaction. The constraints on the range and variety of experiences, ease of movement, and control of the environment have profound effects on the development of children (Lowenfeld, 1981). These effects are most dramatic and debilitating when visual impairments are combined with other disabilities or when the environment is understimulating and nonsocializing. Social and communication problems arise when difficulties in social adjustment, familial problems, or additional developmental handicaps are present.

Social Development.   Fraiberg (1979) and her co-workers have shown how visually impaired infants learn to express attachment. Mutually satisfying interpersonal relationships are established when parents understand and respond to their infants. Instead of eye contact, blind infants use their hands, their bodies, and their voices to establish social contact. Parental attitudes are powerful variables in the social adjustment of children. Social and adjustment problems, immaturity, self-absorption, and other indicators of poor adjustment appear to be related to environmental and experiential factors. Absent or inappropriate feedback about social skills and adverse reactions to their handicaps are associated with problems of adjustment (Van Hasselt & Hersen, 1981).

A sampling of the research indicates that certain aspects of social behavior are clearly more difficult for children with severe visual impairments (Warren, 1984). In a study of vocationally successful young adults, Bauman and Yoder (1966) found that more self-sufficient individuals came from families who were accepting and treated the individual normally. These families did not dwell on the issue of blindness. Self-esteem is derived from the way children are regarded by the people who are important to them. Too much assistance fosters dependency and lowers self-esteem.

Analyses of the interactions between maternal and child behavior show some patterns of differences between visually impaired and sighted groups (Warren, 1984). Immamura (1965) observed that congenitally blind children of dominant mothers accepted the role of followers more readily than sighted children. Mothers' compliance produced more sociable behavior from their blind children, while sighted children demonstrated more dominant behavior in the context of mothers' compliance.

Motor Development.   Among severely visually impaired children with no other disability, there is little delay in motor development until the onset of locomotion (Fraiberg, 1979). Fear of falling, getting lost, or bumping into objects prevents uninhibited exploration of the environment and may interfere with the development of body image. Body image is defined as awareness and control of one's body parts in the execution of movement (Cratty & Sams, 1968). Body concepts are acquired through movement and interaction. For example, awareness of low-hanging branches leads to a lowering of the head when passing underneath. Children who are fearful of movement are deprived of the movement experiences that build body-image concepts (Cratty & Sams, 1968).

A major developmental consequence of severe visual impairment is its impact on mobility. Restricted movement is inevitable unless children are taught to physically negotiate their environments through orientation and mobility training that makes independent travel possible. Choosing where, when, and how to move are taken for granted by people who can see. For the congenitally blind child these choices can only be made when the child has mastered the techniques for traveling without sight. With appropriate instruction in mobility skills, blind children can learn to "travel safely, comfortably, gracefully and independently" (Warren, 1984, p. 103). Teaching orientation and mobility will be discussed in Chapter 7.

Cognitive Development.   Some forms of knowledge are more difficult for visually impaired children to acquire than others. The imagery of congenitally blind people is based on touch and hearing; these modalities do not deliver the same sort of precise information as vision. Some researchers believe that blindness hampers the development of sensorimotor schemes and operational thought (Piaget & Inhelder, 1969; Stephens & Grube, 1982). For example, Stephens and Grube (1982) suggest that congenitally blind children show a marked lag in developing concepts of conservation.

Other writers dispute this belief and maintain that the tasks given to the children were inappropriate and made heavy use of vision (Warren, 1984). Tactual analogues of visual tasks change the nature of the task and do not take into account the differences between tactual and visual information. Vision delivers richly detailed information about form, color, and size. Warren (1984) questioned the validity of some studies that compare blind with sighted children.

Humor and recognition of incongruity are important indices of cognitive development. Rogow (1981a) and Tait and Ward (1982) studied blind children's appreciation of riddles and jokes and found that blind children do not differ from sighted children in their recognition and appreciation of humor. Children's humor closely parallels the development of operational thought (MacDowell, 1979; Schultz, 1974; Whitt & Prentice, 1977). It is clear, however, that action learning is essential to the full development of operational thought. Having an understanding of objects and their uses depends on action learning (Piaget & Inhelder, 1969).

Language Development.   Voice reveals a great deal about people: their size, their location in a room, and their feelings. Voice can be used to identify people and to achieve and maintain social contact. Severely visually impaired children use vocal information even before their speech is fully developed. Many children become adept at interpreting meaning from nuance and variations of vocal tone. Landau (1983), Lenneberg (1967), and others found no substantial differences between blind and sighted children in the acquisition of language. Landau (1983) observed that some word meanings may differ for blind children, but these are related to experiential factors. For example, one blind child used the word "look" to describe the searching activities of the hand rather than the eye.

Neurological Impairments

Given the profound effects of visual handicaps on so many aspects of development, visual impairments in combination with neurological, mental, and hearing handicaps create formidable obstacles to development and learning. Additional handicaps create severe information-gathering problems by further restricting access to sources of stimulation and interfering with the ease of interaction.

Mellor (1979) notes that the frequent association of visual and neurological handicaps, also observed by Tallents (1979), is not surprising, given the close embryological relationship between the brain and the eye. Disorders of the central nervous system, which often include varying degrees of mental retardation, affect from one-third to one-half of the population of visually handicapped children in the Western world (Tallents, 1979; Mellor, 1979).

The delicacy of the infant nervous system renders it susceptible to injury during or before birth. Oxygen deprivation brought about by prolonged labor, precipitate labor, or neonatal cardiac arrest cause a high proportion of the neurological impairments in children (Tallents, 1979; Towbin, 1981). Fetal and neonatal cerebral damage results in abridgment of nervous system function and can lead to cerebral palsy, seizure and behavior disorders, and mental retardation (Towbin, 1981). Cranial hemorrhages that occur during the birth process may also damage the delicate infant optical system (Tallents, 1979). Clinically, these conditions resemble the pathology of stroke in the adult (Towbin, 1981).

Rate of recovery and the potential for recovery are functions of the duration of oxygen deprivation (Nickel & Hoyt, 1982). Short periods of hypoxia (oxygen deprivation) may only result in transient alterations without permanent damage. Intrinsic organic factors such as size and severity of the injury influence the course of recovery (Towbin, 1981). A small area of severe damage may lead to loss of function, whereas mild tissue changes, even though diffuse, may prove reversible. Towbin (1981) emphasizes that external factors, environmental influences, and genetic endowment

> exercise their effects in modifying, increasing, or decreasing cerebral dysfunction following injury. In infants with perinatal complications, as in adults following injury, the subsequent level of function depends to a significant degree on intervention strategies, treatment, environment, social and other tangential factors. (p. 64)

The impact of severe visual handicap on the functioning of children with neurological handicaps is only beginning to be realized. Lack of appropriate stimulation has led to poor prognoses, and poor prognoses have led to low expectations.

Warburg and her co-workers (Warburg, Fredericksen, & Ratleff, 1979) studied blindness among mentally retarded children in Denmark and found a high incidence of neurological impairments among the children. They found that nearly 75% of the children had seizure disorders and 67% had movement disorders such as cerebral palsy. Warburg and her colleagues noted that genetic causes of blindness accounted for the visual handicaps in 60% of nonretarded blind children, whereas only 20% of the blindness among retarded children was related to genetic disorders. Optic atrophy was the leading cause of blindness among the children in Warburg's study.

The fact that the incidence of severe mental handicap is most frequent among the congenitally and totally blind suggests the importance of recognizing the overwhelming constraints caused by the combination of visual impairments with other developmental handicaps. Movement and seizure disorders are the most frequently occurring neurological disorders associated with visual impairments.

Movement Disorders

The most common movement disorder associated with damage to the central nervous system is cerebral palsy. However, movement disorders associated with hypotonia are common among blind children without central nervous system damage (Nickel & Hoyt, 1981).

Movement disorders are generally defined and classified by the characteristics of disordered patterns of movement:

Spasticity is characterized by slow, laborious, and poorly coordinated voluntary movement.

Dyskinesia is characterized by involuntary extraneous motor activity. *Athetoid* movements—uncontrollable, irregular and jerky movements with twisting movements—are among the most striking of dyskinetic movements of the extremities, especially the fingers and wrists (Denhoff, 1979). At times of emotional stress, movements are even more exaggerated.

Ataxia is associated with poor coordination of movements associated with balance, posture, and spatial orientation. It is characterized by inability or awkwardness in the maintenance of balance (Denhoff, 1979).

Mixed types of movement disorders combine dyskinetic, spastic, and ataxic movement patterns.

Hypotonia describes a condition in which the muscles fail to respond to stimulation and deep reflexes may be absent. Hypotonic infants are often described as being "floppy." Hypotonia in infancy may develop into spastic quadriplegia in later childhood (Denhoff, 1979).

Spasticity, the most frequent type of movement disorder, occurs in 50% of the children with cerebral palsy (Denhoff, 1979), while dyskinetic movement disorders, the next in frequency, affect 20 to 25% of them.

Movement disorders are also classified by the number of limbs affected, as seen in the following topographical classification of cerebral palsy (Denhoff, 1979):

Monoplegia: one leg or arm
Biplegia: two limbs
Paraplegia: two legs
Hemiplegia: one side of the body
Quadriplegia: both arms and legs

Age of onset also affects classification: Movement disorders acquired in later childhood as a result of accident or disease are usually not referred to as cerebral palsy, although their effects may be identical.

Seizure (or Convulsive) Disorders

Epilepsy is the general term for chronic seizure disorders and represents the most frequent neurological problems of childhood. Seizures are caused by excessive neuronal discharges (Jabbour, Duenas, Gilmartin, & Gottlieb, 1976). Seizures can affect the whole body or they may be partial; seizure activity may produce psychic, motor, sensory, or visceral phenomena. Jabbour, Duenas, Gilmartin, and Gottlieb (1976) use the categories of the International League Against Epilepsy and classify seizure disorders as follows:

Partial seizures (simple or complex) are focal seizures originating from an abnormal discharge from a localized group of neurons in the brain. The seizure pattern is usually the same from one spell to the next (Berg, 1975). Complex partial seizures involve focal discharges that spread to other regions of the brain and may cause impaired consciousness and be associated with impaired cognition.

Generalized seizures are bilateral and symmetrical. These are grand mal seizures and are dramatic occurrences accompanied by loss of consciousness.

Petit mal seizures are also bilateral. There are different types of petit mal seizure patterns. One type is the staring spell, where there is a suspension of all activity and a clouding of consciousness, but not motor involvement. Another type is the myoclonic attack, a brief contraction of a muscle or groups of muscles. There may be a brief neck flexion or extension in which the head drops forward (Berg, 1975).

Infantile spasms are a form of epilepsy that occurs before the end of the first year of life. Severe forms of infantile spasms are associated with the development of severe movement disorders in later childhood (Berg, 1975).

Unilateral seizures involve only or predominantly one side of the body and may or may not involve impairment of consciousness.

Unclassified disorders form a residual category for disorders about which there is inadequate or incomplete data.

Seizure disorders are symptomatic of underlying nervous system problems. Many children with epilepsy have no other symptomatology; however, seizure disorders are frequent among children with cerebral palsy or other neurological dysfunctions.

Malformations of the Nervous System

The two most commonly occurring primary abnormalities of the central nervous system are *hydrocephalus* and *spina bifida* (Jabbour, Duenas, Gilmartin, & Gottlieb, 1976).

Hydrocephalus: A group of conditions associated with enlargement of the ventricles in the brain. In the majority of instances, hydrocephalus results from obstruction along the cerebrospinal fluid pathways. The clinical signs of hydrocephalus vary depending on age, acuteness of onset, and rapidity of progression. In its acute form there is deterioration of consciousness, disturbances of coordination, and primary optic atrophy. Fortunately the most damaging effects can be prevented with the implantation of a shunt (tube) to drain off excess fluid. Nevertheless, the condition can cause damage to the optic nerve and retina.

Spina Bifida: A congenital midline defect of the spinal column that may occur together with hydrocephalus. In the more severe forms of spina bifida, the spinal cord itself is malformed, causing paralysis of the lower limbs. Malformation of structures within the central nervous system is always associated with neurological impairments; severity, however is variable.

Developmental Consequences

A wide range of behavioral and intellectual problems are associated with neurological disorders. Affected children show too low or too high a threshold for stimulation. Too low a threshold makes it difficult to screen sensory stimuli and results in irritability. Lethargy is a consequence of high thresholds of stimulation; high thresholds place the child at risk for sensory deprivation. Irritable children require a reduction in the type and intensity of stimulation, while lethargic children need an intensification of stimulation.

In general, it is wise to avoid long-term prognoses of children with diagnosed brain damage. As Towbin (1981) observed, levels of function are influenced by environmental and social factors. Rudel (1978) noted that early sensory deprivation may produce symptoms similar to those associated with brain damage, while well-timed intervention may prevent the appearance of a deficit in spite of an early lesion.

Sensory losses and speech and language problems are frequently associated with movement disorders. Motor milestones such as head control, sitting, standing, and walking may be delayed or prevented; as a result, the range of environmental interactions is sharply curtailed. The inability to use one's hands and achieve mastery over physical manipulations interferes with independence skills such as self-feeding and self-dressing.

Passivity is fostered by physical dependence. Like severe visual handicaps, physical handicaps impose severe limitations on experience and interaction. In general, the developmental consequences of neurological impairments are related to the following variables (Denhoff, 1979):

Type of movement disorder
Degree of severity
Presence or absence of other disabilities
Availability of intervention services
Family attitudes and expectations

The developmental consequences of seizure disorders depend on the severity and types of associated disorders, rather than on the presence of seizure activity alone. Most children and adults with seizure disorders can and do function normally when their seizures are medically controlled. However, when seizure disorders are associated with movement and sensory disorders, affected children are likely to show other developmental disabilities.

Mental Handicaps and Developmental Disabilities

Mental retardation is too easily assumed for children who are multiply handicapped. Functional mental retardation may be the consequence rather than a cause of impaired social, language, and cognitive performance. Understimulation, experiential deprivation, and inability to act on the environment produce an emotional lethargy that disguises mental ability. The preferred term, *developmental disability,* will be used here. Nevertheless, it is important to review the definitions and concepts of mental retardation that are in common use.

Definitions and Classification

From a functional perspective, mental retardation is difficult to define as a clinical entity. The term "mental retardation" itself is a hypothetical construct that leaves "room for much debate regarding the best method of defining this phenomenon" (Seltzer, 1983, p. 144). Functional, noncategorical definitions of mental retardation emphasize the relationships between the individual and the environment. The term "developmental disabilities" takes into account the environmental conditions that may be contributing to retarded levels of functioning (Seltzer, 1983).

Developmental disabilities are severe and chronic disorders attributable to mental or physical impairments or combinations of mental and physical impairments. Developmental disabilities occur prior to adulthood and result in substantial limitations in three or more of the following (Seltzer, 1983):

Self-care
Language development
Learning
Mobility
Self-direction
Capacity for independent living
Economic self-sufficiency

While the term "developmental disabilities" lacks operational clarity, it does not carry the stigma attached to mental retardation. A widely accepted categorical definition is that given by the American Association on Mental Deficiency (AAMD). According to this definition, mental retardation is subaverage general intellectual functioning that originates during the developmental period and is combined with deficits in adaptive behavior (Seltzer, 1983). A low IQ score and deficits in adaptive behavior are two elements that define mental retardation.

The American Association on Mental Deficiency recognizes four levels or categories of mental retardation, as determined by scores achieved on intelligence tests (Seltzer, 1983).

Level of MR	IQ Score
mild	56–70
moderate	41–55
severe	26–40
profound	25 and below

Adaptive behavior is the ability of individuals to meet the standards of personal independence and social responsibility expected of their age and cultural groups (Seltzer, 1983). Adaptive behaviors include communication, social, and mastery skills. Measures of adaptive behavior accompany assessments of intelligence.

Developmental Consequences

Severe visual impairments in combination with even mild levels of mental retardation conceal the potential of children beneath depressed levels of functioning. Understimulation, sensory deprivation, impaired mobility, and lack of affective relationships cause many blind children to appear to be moderately or even severely retarded. Woodcock (1974) observed that many blind retarded children successfully manipulate their environments by their inactivity. By shutting out the world, they avoid stimulation and the need to make a response. There is no contingency between their actions and the environment, which provides for their basic needs, food, clothing and shelter.

Visually impaired developmentally handicapped children often display an unevenness in their development and may well have islands of intact function. Their responsiveness to intervention is a far better indicator of their potential functioning than their scores on intelligence tests are. In children with neurological disorders and/or hearing impairments, mental retardation may be both consequence and cause of developmental problems. Lack of normal interactions may also be the consequence of severe visual handicaps combined with hearing impairments.

Hearing Impairments

Hearing impairments are caused by interference with the transmission of sound from the ear to the brain and vary from mild to profound. Children who are deaf are unable to hear spoken language with or without hearing aids. Hard-of-hearing children are generally able to hear spoken language with the use of hearing aids. Hearing impairments are classified according to the degree of hearing loss as measured on a decibel scale (see Table 3.1). (A decibel is the smallest difference in sound intensity that can be detected by the human ear.)

The most severe hearing impairments are caused by sensorineural problems that interfere with the transmission of auditory nerve impulses to the brain (Moores, 1978). Such sensorineural problems are frequently associated with other neurological impairments and ac-

TABLE 3.1. Levels of Hearing Impairment

Severity	Hearing threshold decibel range	Consequence
Mild	25–40 dB	Difficulty hearing conversation in group settings
Moderate	40–60 dB	Frequent difficulty with normal speech
Severe	60–90 dB	Speech seems faint or distorted; requires amplification
Profound	90 dB	Cannot hear speech even with amplification

count for the majority of hearing problems experienced by visually impaired children.

The term *deaf/blind* is widely applied to individuals with combined hearing and sight problems. Classifications of children in this category are broad and flexible to allow the greatest number to have access to specialized services. In fact, however, most of the children in this category have residual vision and hearing and thus are actually neither deaf nor blind. Functional definitions of deaf/blindness stress the type of programs needed rather than the condition of the child. Kirk and Gallagher (1979) define deaf/blind children as those in whom the combination of visual and auditory impairments causes "such severe communication and other developmental and educational problems that they cannot properly be accommodated in special education programs either for the hearing handicapped child or for the visually handicapped child" (Kirk & Gallagher, 1979, p. 437).

Rubella (German measles) deserves special mention because it has been a major cause of combined visual and hearing loss in children. Although degrees of severity vary greatly, the more severe forms include neurological and cardiac difficulties in addition to sensory impairments (Lemeshow, 1982). Bilateral cataracts are the most common visual handicap among rubella children. Studies of the ocular manifestations of rubella indicate that cataracts caused by the rubella virus are often associated with microphthalmia, retinal disease, and nystagmus (Van Dijk, 1982). The most significant visual disorder apart from cataracts is nystagmus.

Characteristics of multisensory-impaired children may include retardation of physical development, low scores on developmental scales, apathy, minimum of smiling, rejection of physical contact, and limited interaction between the child and the environment. Stereotyped and self-stimulating behavior are frequently observed among this population (Van Dijk, 1982). These behaviors include light gazing (a sign that the child does have some sight), hand flapping, sensitivities to sound and odor, whirling, and jumping (Van Dijk, 1982). Behaviorally, some children show characteristics associated with childhood autism. Although many writers caution against the use of the term "autism" when talking about visually impaired children with additional handicaps, it is a difficult term to avoid because it is used so frequently in descriptions of their behavior.

Another major cause of multisensory impairments is Usher's syndrome, characterized by sensorineural deafness and retinitis pigmentosa. The onset of retinitis pigmentosa usually appears in later childhood or adolescence. Because children with Usher's syndrome have vision in their developing years, the effects on personality development are not as global as is the case with rubella. Children with sensorineural deafness should be frequently examined by an eye care professional for early detection of retinitis pigmentosa.

Conclusion

Definitions and classifications of handicaps identify and describe handicapping conditions, not the individuals who have those conditions. Similarly, diagnostic categories do not define developmental, social, or educational needs. The developmental consequences of complex handicaps depend on environmental factors as much as on the handicaps themselves. The children behind the labels are individuals with personalities, styles of learning, and needs that are as individual as their fingerprints. In order to override the often overwhelming effects of complex handicaps, the children must be helped to establish contact and interaction with their social and physical worlds. Developmental tasks of the early years are made more complex and difficult to master by the presence of visual and other handicapping conditions. It may take longer for individual children to learn those things that seem to be acquired quickly and effortlessly by their nonhandicapped peers.

The purpose of this chapter has been to understand the impact of visual handicaps in combination with other disabilities on human growth and learning. The remaining chapters will address the needs of children as they learn to cope with the demands of becoming full-fledged participants in their families and in society.

4.

Learning to Be:
The Foundation of Education

Intimate interactions with other people are a necessary condition for the formation of a "self" capable of acting with independence and purpose. Interaction powers the drive towards self-realization. Active encounters with people and objects give meaning and substance to all domains of learning. In the preceding chapters we have introduced and defined the concept of dynamic interaction, addressed the beginnings of the interactive process in infancy, and described the effects that visual handicaps, alone or in combination with other handicapping conditions, have on environmental interactions. The present chapter addresses the emergence of "self," including the body self, in relation to sensorimotor learning. The development of hand function and object manipulation is also included because this area is so important to visually impaired individuals.

Bruner (1966) observed that children become interested in doing those things that they become good at doing. This simple truth is a good way to introduce a chapter concerned with helping children acquire basic mastery skills. Accurate and humane assessment of the children who are the subject of this book requires a rejection of simplistic concepts of cognitive development and rigid notions of learning hierarchies. Observing the progress that is possible in their struggles toward competence and independence offers different views of the landscapes of human learning.

Learning defies precise definition because it is so much a part of human existence; it is as basic a function as breathing or eating. Learning can be described as becoming aware, adapting, changing, participating, and acquiring knowledge and skills. Making sense of the world is the foundation on which cognition is built (Piaget, 1958). MacNamara (1972) suggested that children are able to learn language precisely because of a well-developed capacity for making sense of situations involving direct and immediate human interaction.

The process of environmental interaction requires a "self," an active "I" that is eager, willing, and able to act. M. Donaldson (1978) in describing the role of awareness, stated that if children are to develop their intellectual powers, they must gain some control over their own thinking. Before they can gain control, they must become aware. As Donaldson observed, control over thinking means a movement beyond simple experience of sensation to the construction of ideas based on experience.

> The attaining of this control means prising thought out of its primitive unconscious embeddedness in the immediacies of living in the world and interacting with other human beings. It means learning to move beyond the bounds of human sense. It is on this movement that all higher intellectual skills depend. (p. 123)

Becoming aware begins with awareness of having a separate and independent self that is conscious of its separateness and independence and knows what it feels and experiences. The self plans actions and controls thought. The idea of "self" incorporates a notion of the "body self" as the agent of its actions. As sensations are experienced and associated with events in the external environment, the self as a separate entity begins to take form. Self is first realized on a concrete level with awareness of sensation and ability to act upon the environment: The self is an explorer and user of objects.

Doug's experience illustrates the nature of the difficulties faced by a passive child in realizing a self capable of influencing his environment. Doug is a congenitally blind developmentally delayed 8-year-old. There are seven children in his class. At circle time, the teacher plays her guitar and the children sing. Doug knows the words of the song perfectly. His voice is pure and musical. He sings the song with the others. Now the teacher asks the children to talk about something that they especially enjoy doing.

"Swimming," "eating candy," "playing games," say a chorus of voices. Doug, no longer listening, rocks back and forth in his chair. "How about you, Doug?" asks the teacher. Doug does not answer. "Doug likes to eat cake," offers another child.

The teacher laughs and moves close to Doug. She puts her hand on his shoulder and asks again. "What is fun for you, Doug?"

"Fun for Doug, fun for Doug," says Doug in a monotone voice. "I don't want to be in fun. Big boys shouldn't be in fun," he adds tonelessly.

Children like Doug present a very mixed profile of abilities and disabilities. On the one hand, there is his verbal ability; he speaks clearly and in sentences. On the other hand is the paucity of his language, which is unlinked to purpose or activity. His auditory skills are finely tuned. He loves music, has perfect pitch, and can remember the words and melodies of many songs. But his gross and fine motor skills are seriously delayed. Objects hold little interest for him; his hands hang by his sides inert and lifeless, neither exploring nor manipulating objects. When he walks, he tilts his head to one side, and moves with great caution as if he were afraid of tripping on his feet. Doug clings fearfully to a wall when walking by himself, preferring to be guided by an adult. His body is slouched when he stands and sits. Left alone, he sits or stands and rocks his body back and forth.

Doug floats in a timeless world and rarely expresses personal desire. The unevenness in his development is observed in his hand function. Although he rarely explores or manipulates objects, he can read words in braille. He reads with only one finger, but he knows the braille alphabet and can read single words and short sentences. His reading is slow and laborious, and unless his teacher is sitting by his side, he makes no effort to read alone. His skills are not directed to definable purposes or goals.

Observing Doug yields a number of insights into the effects of a self-image devoid of any sense of control over events. One day, for example, Doug bent his head to get a drink from a water fountain that was recessed in a wall. As he raised up after drinking, he bumped his head against the wall. Doug then shouted in frustrated anger, "I hate it when I do that to myself," and, with those words, punched himself hard in the chest. On another occasion, Doug showed that he did not feel himself to be an actor in the environment. Doug and three other boys were working on a puppet play. As he sat with the other children, Doug ignored their talk and laughter, his puppet hanging lifelessly on his hand. "My puppet won't talk," he said with great disappointment. "Give me a puppet that talks," he said.

After several weeks of working with the puppets, his teacher observed that Doug began to rock his puppet back and forth, instead of his own body. This was the first time that Doug communicated through a puppet.

Body Image and the Notion of "Self"

The centrality of body image to learning was stressed by Guldager (1970), who noted that "without knowledge of one's body, it is very difficult, if not indeed impossible, to gain knowledge of other things" (p. 43). Body image is a construct, a concept formed of the body self through a variety of physical experiences. Physical actions result in physical sensations—sensations of movement, of touch, of being still or of being active (Schantz, 1969). The body "self" is realized with thousands of physical actions on the environment. The body self is the agent of transactions with the environment (Williams, 1983). If children are unable to control or will their body selves to controlled actions, they experience selves that are passive and powerless. This experience of self is the body image or body concept.

The body image is a composite of body experiences; the greater the variety of experience, the more stable and comprehensive the body image. Van der Velde (1985) observed that the physical self is the only medium for human psychological transactions, verbal and nonverbal. He suggested that body image is a composite of multiple images, derived from multiple experiences, which serve as "mental blueprints for the organization of social behavior" (p. 527).

Dr. Oliver Sacks (1984), noted neurologist and researcher, observed that severe body image disturbances are inevitably accompanied by disturbances of the body ego. Describing the effects of neurological trauma or disease, Sacks wrote that body image disturbances are experienced as "a radical collapse of action, the radical collapse of experience, the radical collapse of their 'categories,' elemental space and time" (1984, p. 167).

A sampling of the psychological and neurological research on body image suggests that there is a fundamental relationship between body image, sensory integration, and the ability to act on the environment. In the following section a number of studies that indicate these relationships are reviewed.

Evidence from Body Image Research

Schantz (1969), a psychologist who spent many years researching body image, proposed that body image develops from both the sensory and motor aspects of experiencing the body in motion. According to Schantz, the most fundamental form of body experience is the experience of the body as a single object with a specific locus in space. The ability to plan the outcome of specific motor actions (motor planning) is based on body image. Schantz (1969) classified body experiences into a hierarchy of motor actions:

Level I: Basic functions, such as eating, drinking, and walking
Level II: Refinement of gross and fine motor activities
Level III: Skilled movements such as writing, painting, and
    sculpturing
Level IV: Total body mastery, such as ballet and gymnastics

Self-identification occurs after the physical self has been globally realized (Schantz, 1969). For example, it becomes possible to think in terms of "up or down" or "near or far" only after spatial localization of the body has been achieved. In a 1978 study, Gilbert, Finell and Young found that there was a significant relationship between body concepts and imagination among 69 kindergarten children. Williams (1983) noted that a stable body image is the basis of well-coordinated movement and that well-coordinated movement enhances body image.

Body image is so central to normal development that the consequences of distortion are dramatic. As Schantz and others have noted, the importance of body image becomes evident in circumstances that impede or distort its formation. Sangorvin (1977) studied 48 10-year-olds with polio and scoliosis. His study showed a significant relationship between the type of disorder and type of body image distortion.

The range of differences between actuality and perception can be glimpsed by looking at examples of opposite but equivalent body image distortions. For instance, persons who have experienced the amputation of an arm or leg report a "phantom limb"; they feel the limb as if it were still attached to their bodies. Gross and Melzack (1978) were able to produce a phantom limb experience in noninjured people after 40 minutes of the application of a pressure cuff on the arm. By contrast, injuries to the central or peripheral nervous system that result in loss of sensation in an arm or leg can produce severe disturbance of body image that is the reverse of the phantom limb; patients with this condition report feelings of the loss of the limb, as if it had "disappeared."

Difficulties in finger localization are sometimes used as an index of body image disorders (Benton, 1979a; Van Dijk, 1982). Benton (1979a) observed that body image is more than knowing the names of body parts. Some children can name their body parts and still be unsuccessful localizing the position of objects in space. Cratty and Sams (1968) investigated body image in blind children and concluded that movement is an essential variable in the achievement of free and uninhibited mobility.

Body image problems express themselves in a variety of sensory and perceptual disorders. Gerstmann (1958), one of the early writers to classify body image problems, proposed the following categories:

1. Inability to visually recognize faces or objects even after repeated exposure and familiarity. Perceptual disorders may include feelings of disorientation to parts of the body, such as the fingers.

2. Perceptual disorders associated with hemiplegia (paralysis of one half of the body). People with this condition may have difficulty recognizing sensory stimuli on one side of the body.
3. Phantom limb experiences associated with amputation of an arm or leg. The individual perceives the missing limb as if it were still present. The phantom limb experience is important for learning to use prostheses.
4. Disorders manifested in abnormal somatic sensations and perceptions. Eating disorders such as anorexia nervosa belong to this category.
5. Disorders experienced in dream states.

Considerations in Assessment of Body Image Concepts

Body image depends on physical as well as psychological factors. Ayres (1972) suggested that the quality of muscle tone is an important consideration. As discussed in the previous chapter, the hypotonia often associated with congenital blindness may be caused by inactivity or may be a symptom of neurological impairment. Distractibility and hyperactivity can also be associated with equilibrium problems. Obsessive movement, such as stereotypic rocking, is likely to be associated with poor sensory integration.

Deformities, contractures, or atrophy of muscles can affect postural control and thus interfere with control of movement. Children who ignore parts of their bodies such as their hands, or who have a weakness or paralysis on one side of the body, experience problems in integrating body parts. Integration of body parts, needed for a stable body image, cannot occur when body parts are ignored (Ayres, 1972). Difficulty in establishing a stable body image should be suspected in children who have persistent primitive reflexes and difficulty in maintaining postural equilibrium.

Fearfulness and lethargy are also indicators of body image problems. The fearfulness of some children may reflect their postural insecurity. Children who experience even mild impairments of equilibrium exhibit fear responses in many movement situations, such as riding in an elevator. Poor health and lack of stamina, and the body image problems they entail, are often expressed by lethargy and an inability to engage in or sustain physical activity.

The failure of laterality—left or right hemispheric dominance—to emerge interferes with the organization of skilled movement. The phenomenon of laterality affects both language development and hand preference, and also, though to a lesser extent, preference in the use of eye, ear, and foot (Lenneberg, 1967).

Lack of variety of movement patterns, unusual or atypical physical responses to environmental stimuli (such as holding the hands over the ears), inequality of movement on each side of the body, lack of coordinated movement, difficulty in localizing objects, insecurity in walking, and inefficient manual function are all indications of problems in body image (Connor, Williamson, & Siepp, 1978).

Sensorimotor Learning

The importance of the body image construct resides in its relation to the process of sensorimotor learning. The dimensions of self, including body image, are fashioned out of the quality of the social and physical interaction with one's environment. Ideas about the body are fashioned out of the perceptions of body experiences—bodily sensations experienced internally and externally. The proprioceptive, visual, and equilibrium senses are of particular importance in developing a sense of the body (Sacks, 1985). Normally, these sensory systems work together; however, if one of the systems is not working, the others must compensate. In an important sense it is impossible to talk of body image without also talking about sensorimotor learning.

As the term implies, sensorimotor learning involves being able to interpret sensation and make an appropriate motor response. Becoming aware of and interpreting meaning from sensation are the beginning steps of environmental awareness. Psychological adaptation to the environment demands the ability to interpret sensory information in order to organize increasingly complex responses. Accurate interpretation of sensory information depends on the ability of the brain to:

Receive sensation
Be aware of sensation
Integrate past with present sensation (memory)
Interpret sensation (assign meaning to sensory experience)

Sensory Integration

Sensation comes to the brain both from within the body and from the external world. Internal sensations arising from the body itself are thermal (temperature sense), proprioceptive, and visceral (Van der Velde, 1985). External sensations come from outside the body and are transmitted through the eyes, the ears, the mouth, the nose, and the hands. Vision and audition, the distal senses, bring sensory information from outside the body. Unvarying or constant sensations are only noticed in conditions of change. For example, temperature or air pressure make themselves known only when they change or become extreme.

Sensation reaches conscious awareness only when the brain acknowledges it. And while sensations are rarely experienced in isolation from one another, the human brain analyzes and organizes sensory information according to the way it is received. Sensation is not simply the passive receiving of sense impressions; the experience of sensation is the result of highly organized sensory systems capable of receiving, interpreting, and acting on the sensory information. Sensory systems, such as the visual or auditory system, act in concert with other sensory modalities. The sensory systems or modalities on which sensorimotor learning is based are generally classified as

Audition: the sense of hearing

Gustatory: the sense of taste

Olfactory: the sense of smell

Proprioceptive: the sensory system that helps to regulate posture by informing the brain about the position of the body and its parts

Tactile: the sense of touch, including both an active and a passive mode. The active mode includes contact, exploration, and manipulation and is most often experienced through the hands. The passive mode refers to sensations that are received incidentally, such as rubbing a child's hands to awaken awareness.

Vestibular: The second positional sense, which informs the brain about the body in motion, gravity, and balance. Kinesthesia is another term for the sensation of the body in motion.

Visual: the sense of sight. Together with audition it provides the most efficient information about the environment. The visual system will be discussed in more detail in Chapter 7.

Sensory integration is the ability to connect and associate sensations; the integration of sensory information permits the formation of realistic and predictable notions of the world outside of the body. The process of sensory integration begins before birth and is refined through experience. Consider the following vignette.

Jane is playing in the garden. Suddenly she hears a clap of thunder and catches a glimpse of a flash of lightning. Quickly, Jane gathers up her playthings and runs indoors just before the heavy downpour. Once indoors, Jane rushes to the window to watch the downpour of rain.

Jane's knowledge of the meaning of environmental events enabled her to make the appropriate response. Her association of thunder (sound) with lightning and the darkening clouds (sight) led to the interpretation (rainstorm). The downpour (feedback) verified Jane's perception and consolidated her understanding. Four important elements may be identified in this sequence of events:

Stimulus reception: thunder (sound), lightning and rainclouds (sight)
Sensory integration: meaning derived from 2 or more senses (thunderstorm)
Motor response: decision about how to act, what to do
Feedback: rainstorm

Movement is a powerful organizer of sensorimotor experiences. Sensory integration allows co-occurring sensory events to be fused in a single integrated experience (Ayres, 1972). Movement plays a special role in the self-realization of congenitally blind children. Fraiberg (1977) demonstrated that blind children form notions of object permanence. As they learn to move independently within the environment and explore objects, they become efficient in recognizing and discriminating objects. Before considering the alterations in neurosensory development that sensory impairment may impose, it is helpful to examine the sequences of normal neurosensory development. The best source for such an overview comes from neuroevolutionary theory.

Neuroevolutionary Theory

Sensorimotor learning is characterized by a hierarchy of increasingly complex functions. Through the course of a spiraling number of sensorimotor experiences, children construct ideas about themselves and the external world and test them in thousands of action events. Actions and interactions become more complex as children are increasingly able to integrate and associate sensory information and motor responses.

Neuroevolutionary theory maintains that complex functions are based upon the acquisition and mastery of simpler functions (Mysak, 1980; Ayres, 1972). According to Mysak (1980), in the development of the human brain, there has been a "progressive incorporation of lower brains by higher ones and the subsequent control, modification, and elaboration of all behaviors associated with earlier or lower brains by the highest or latest to evolve brain" (p. 24).

In Mysak's (1980) view, the concept of progressive integration and elaboration is the essence of development. Each stage in the progression of development is built upon the accomplishments of preceding stages. For example, reflex responses to environmental stimuli become highly controlled voluntary responses as infants gain control of their physical movement and acquire skill in interactions with their environments.

As the brain develops, its higher centers coordinate and control lower centers (Ayres, 1972). In the process of evolution, the cortex, the most evolved portion of the human brain, incorporated the control and maintenance of both upright posture and the skilled movements of arms and hands (Bobath, 1985). Neuroevolutionary theorists argue that the stages in the evolutionary development of the human brain are reflected in the sequential emergence of human skills in the individual (Ayres, 1972).

At each level there is organization of function that enables function at higher, or cortical, levels. External stimuli play an important role in the establishment of each successive level of organization (Ayres, 1972). Motor learning occurs most effectively when the normal sequence of development can be followed (Ayres, 1972; Mysak, 1980).

Sensorimotor learning has two aspects: the ability of the brain to receive sensory stimuli and the ability to make a motor response. Sensory integration mediates the relationships between the two aspects. Research on both human and animal brain function has demonstrated that there are specific neuronal assemblies in the brain where sensory integration occurs; the Hyvarinens (1982), for example, identified the sensory integration functions of the association cortex of the parietal lobe.

Sensory integration may be delayed or even prevented in conditions of immaturity of or damage to the nervous system. For example, the integration of proprioceptive and vestibular sensations, which is essential to postural control and postural security, may not develop in children with severe movement disorders because too little sensory information is available to the brain.

Sensory Deprivation

The brain is nourished by receiving and integrating a steady stream of sensory stimulation, especially the sensations arising from the body itself (Ayres, 1972). The effect of too little stimulation is to rob the brain of the information it requires in order to interpret the world. Lack of sensory experience and sensation-generating movement deprives the brain of its ability to integrate the proprioceptive and vestibular sensory systems, thus preventing the emergence of a stable body image. Clinically the effects of diminished sensory stimulation are difficulty in organizing and interpreting sensory information and relating self to objects and objects to other objects (Ayres, 1972).

Interaction within the environment is a primary source of sensory information and sensory feedback. Children who are not actively engaged in interaction within their environments inevitably experience a reduction in the quantity and quality of sensory experience. Diminished sensory input denies the brain the sensory feedback it requires for active perception and interpretation of environmental events. Without the feedback that comes from normal activity, perception cannot develop in a normal way (Gardner, 1983).

Sensory deprivation resulting from too little sensory stimulation causes a plummeting in the brain's efficiency to interpret sensory information. Injury to the nervous system can lead to sensory deprivation by preventing the integration of sensory input. For example, injury at the level of the spinal cord or brain stem may cause incoming sensation to be "drained off" and thus not allow "the child to manifest all of his sensorimotor potential" (Mysak, 1980, p. 195).

In order to efficiently compensate for the loss of sight, a child needs a continuous supply of sensation from the other sense modalities. Continuous information from other sense modalities makes it possible for blind children to construct meaningful ideas about their environments. Modalities such as touch and hearing become the primary source of information about the world outside of the body. Hearing supplies a great deal of information, but unless hearing is combined with other sense modalities, the information it carries is incomplete. For example, imagine listening to the sound of traffic without knowing its source; the constant rush of the wheels, the sound of the horns, the squeal of brakes are empty of meaning until tied to a source.

The environment is full of meaningless and disturbing sounds, and some children respond by learning to tune them out. Unfortunately learning to ignore disturbing sounds means ignoring other sounds as well. Children ignore the information they experience as meaningless. Ignoring external stimuli leads to a reduction in the quantity and quality of sensory experience.

Hyvarinen and Hyvarinen (1982) proposed a physiological basis for ignoring visual stimuli: Early visual deprivation leads to the inability of neural tissue to make normal use of visual signals. The result is reduced visual input to these portions of the brain that integrate vision with other sense modalities, such as hearing or touch. There is a decrease in the representation of vision in the associative systems of the brain (Hyvarinen & Hyvarinen, 1982). Sonksen (1982) found that when vision is virtually absent in one eye and limited in the other there may be unbalanced levels of integration of auditory inputs from each ear, resulting in difficulties in sound localization. Van Dijk (1982) found that the effects of diminished vision on the functioning of children with rubella were greater than the effects of other developmental problems.

The construction of sensible ideas about the environment depends initially on the quality of sensory experience. Adaptive responses are acts of judgment based on skills in interpreting sensory information. To hear the patter of rain and know that it is raining outdoors, to smell the fragrance of baking bread and know that bread is baking in an oven are the products of linking what the senses discern to the real events associated with them.

Children make their own adaptations to their environments as they learn the meanings of the sensory events they experience. Adaptive responses are signs of recognition of meaning and of the need for acting. The reasons for acting become clear when their effects can be predicted. There is little source of meaning for children who cannot see the world and who do not venture to feel it, to explore and touch it. Without environmental interaction, the world becomes uninviting, an alien and unknowable place. It is little wonder that such children do not make adaptive adjustments to a place perceived as unknown and unknowable.

The depth of isolation of such children is revealed in their poor mobility, their stereotypic mannerisms, such as rocking and echolalic language, and their limp and inactive hands. Rocking movements produce internal sensations but they do not lead to explorations of surrounding space. The absence of interaction creates conditions of sensory deprivation and a resulting poverty of experience. These children are cast adrift in a sea of confused and meaningless sense impressions. As Sacks (1984) noted, a radically defective experience must be assumed to have consequences for both inner states and perceptions of the external world.

Sensory Stimulation and Awareness of Self

Sensory awareness is the first step towards realizing a "self" able to act, adapt, adjust, and enjoy being alive. Self-awareness is the essence of purposeful action and enjoyment of discovery. In the absence of "selfhood," children may acquire skills, but these skills remain undeveloped, fragmented, unintegrated, and unrelated to purpose. Raising awareness changes the child's way of experiencing (Boxill, 1985). The process is one of moving from passive to active experiencing, a concept analogous to Carl Rogers' (1961) observation that as the individual becomes more self-aware, he becomes free to change and grow.

There are two essential steps in developing awareness of sensation. The first is embellishment of sensation at the level of input. Augmenting or highlighting sensory experiences cultivates awareness. Augmentation is achieved by increasing the intensity of the stimulus or by combining sensory stimuli. For example, using music or rhythm together with movement combines auditory with proprioceptive and tactile stimuli. Dimension highlighting is another way of describing sensory enhancement. Sensory enhancement must lead to meaningful interpretation. This is the reason music therapy is so effective in developing sensory awareness.

The second step of sensory awareness is feedback. The feedback phase of sensory experience is necessary in order to develop awareness of sensation. Motor thinking, motor planning, and motor control are dependent on feedback. Feedback encourages purposive actions because it makes them predictable. For example, if children know that when they splash in water, they will get wet, they approach water play with just that objective in mind. Feedback validates the sensory experience. Feedback also has an important role in the development of motor control and motor learning (Mysak, 1980).

Connor, Williamson, and Siepp (1978) noted that sensory stimulation is the major principle of intervention with hypotonic children. Choice, variety, and intensity of stimulation should be tailored to individual needs. Before a developmental skill can be mastered and generalized to new situations, it must first be learned.

Consistent and continuous therapeutic interventions and sensory stimulation help to establish basic body concepts and establish patterns of interaction. Neurodevelopmental therapy contributes to the building of the neurophysiological links on which motor learning is based. The skills and the support of a variety of professionally trained workers are essential components of comprehensive educational and treatment programs. The reader is referred to the work of Bobath (1985) for detailed information about neurodevelopmental therapy.

Visual stimulation should be an integral part of any program of sensory development for children who have some degree of sight or for whom diagnoses of vision are problematic. In normally sighted children, the sense of sight is well-organized and integrated with other

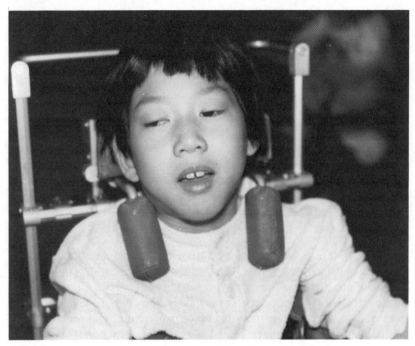

Learning to look: Mimi begins to direct her gaze

sense modalities such as hearing, touch, and kinesthesia (movement). A well-organized visual system is expressed with visual behaviors such as visual attention, gaze, search, recognition of human faces and familiar objects, and eye–hand–coordinated movements. The integration of the hand and eye is the basis of a broad range of skills (Hass, 1985).

The absence of perfect sight does not mean that the visual system cannot be utilized for environmental information. Approximately 75–80% of all school-age visually handicapped children have some usable vision (Barraga, 1976). Unusual behaviors such as finger flicking in front of lights or hand waving indicate that the child has some vision, as does the fascination with lights observed in young rubella children with growing cataract density by Van Dijk (1982).

The goal of vision stimulation is to help children find meaning in visual stimuli. The visual system is flexible and can be reorganized with visual input early in life. The physiological capacity of nerve cells to respond to sensory stimuli can be strengthened with sensory stimulation (Fellows, Leguire, Rogers, & Bremer, 1986). The response properties of vision cells demonstrate a remarkable increase with stimulation. Age appears to be the key variable in the reversal of the effects of vision deprivation in the case of amblyopia in children (Assaf, 1982). In a pioneering study, Barraga (1964) found that visual stimulation improves visual efficiency among school-age children with severe visual impairments. The younger the child when vision stimulation begins, the better. Vision enhancement is an educational intervention designed to enable children to utilize their remaining vision as a learning channel. As such it is an important component of special education for visually impaired children and will be discussed in detail in Chapter 7.

Educational Interventions

The aim of education in the domain of sensorimotor learning is to awaken the senses as pathways to the mind. The skills associated with sensorimotor development and gross and fine motor development are intimately linked with the skills of acting on the world and include mastery and coping skills. Learning in the sensorimotor area brings children into contact with themselves and their environments. Sensorimotor learning takes place within the context of environmental interactions. The next portion of this chapter is devoted to discussion of educational approaches that are as much concerned with the establishment of a context for interaction as with the development of individual skills. Indeed, the reader is already familiar with the inventory of sensorimotor skills in the domain of sensorimotor learning. Co-active methods are directed towards the encouragement of motivation and participation as much as skill development. These methods, represented by music therapy and co-active movement theory as developed by Van Dijk, are tailored to the needs of noninteracting children.

Instruction for children who are "tuned out" and "turned off" is far more than a curriculum or a set of activities designed to teach skills and concepts. Co-active approaches are as concerned with establishing trust relationships as they are with eventual learning outcomes. The usefulness of these approaches lies in the willingness of teachers to work at the level of the children in order to bring them out of their isolation.

Common to all co-active interventions is the way adults relate to children. The term *co-active* refers to the role of the adults as partners and sharers of experience. Within the context of co-action, adults are models of interactive behaviors, not authority figures.

Music Therapy

Music and musical activities are vivid, intelligible experiences by themselves and require no abstract thought. As Nordoff and Robbins (1985) point out,

> Music is a universal experience in the sense that all can share in it; its fundamental elements of melody, harmony, and rhythm appeal to, and engage their related psychic functions in each one of us. Music is also universal in that its message, the content of its expression, can encompass all heights and depths of human experience, all shades of feeling. (p. 15).

Even in children in whom the sense of self may be only a dim awareness, music can stimulate emotions and activities to propel them into the external world (Boxill, 1985). The inherent qualities of music, the rhythms and melodies, engage the attention of children, thus making musical activities an ideal medium to achieve contact. As Nordoff and Robbins (1985) noted, to the degree that music can reach hard to reach children, musical experience becomes music therapy.

Sarah's experience illustrates how musical activities (musical therapy) can help to develop self-awareness. Sarah was 6 years old when she was enrolled in a special program for developmentally handicapped children. The combination of bilateral cataracts, nystagmus, a suspected hearing loss, and a mild form of spasticity in her lower body made Sarah a severely handicapped little girl. She was easily frustrated and uninterested in her surroundings. Light, both natural light and lamplight, attracted her interest, but instead of exploring, she gazed at the light, standing in one spot and flapping her hand in front of one eye while staring at a light bulb. Her movements were poorly coordinated, although she walked independently in small, hopping steps. She had sufficient sight to move around the environment without fear of falling or bumping into objects. Sarah did not speak or use signs and resisted holding new and unfamiliar objects in her hands. She used her hand as if it were a clamp, holding objects between her thumb and four stiff fingers. She had not been observed to flex or work with her fingers.

A music therapist who came weekly to Sarah's school began working with her. The first time Sarah responded to musical activities was when the music therapist, holding a small drum, followed Sarah around the room, playing the drum in time to Sarah's movements. Sarah came close and tentatively placed her hand on the drum. The therapist gave Sarah a tambourine, but Sarah let it fall from her hand. She was more interested in listening to the teacher's drum. After a short time, Sarah again approached the therapist. This time she varied her movements, walking quickly and then slowly, as if to test if it was her movements that caused the drumbeats to be slow or fast. Then she approached the therapist again and reached for the drum.

Sarah was encouraged to explore the drum and produce any sounds she wished. Sarah made tentative tapping motions and then banged hard on the drum. Taking another drum, the therapist imitated Sarah's sounds and developed a musical conversation with a smiling Sarah, who began to initiate drum conversations. In the therapist's words, "Sarah had connected."

In music therapy, sensorimotor deficits that have prevented or restricted interaction with the environment are dealt with directly through the sensorimotor stimulation of music-movement (Boxill, 1985). Rhythms help the child to focus on external stimuli and organize motor responses. Changes in tempo arouse the detached child (Boxill, 1985). By linking rhythm with movement, music therapy helps children to organize their physical movements.

> When we live in the tonal and temporal structures of a musical composition—as children do when they play instruments in it—our participation integrates our responding faculties. It is out of this completeness of the relationship between music and the human being that music therapy in its truest sense arises. (Nordoff & Robbins, 1985, p. 17)

By working with children either singly or in small groups, the therapist invites the child to enter new domains of experience. Introducing children to the use of simple musical instruments creates interest in objects. Blind children with severe multiple handicaps attain surprisingly high levels of musical competence and begin to create their own music. Music therapy is effective in awakening a sense of being and achievement in severely withdrawn children.

Co-active Movement Theory

Co-active movement theory, as formulated by Van Dijk (1968, 1982), is a more structured approach to enable noninteractive children to establish relationships with their teachers and develop communication. Van Dijk developed his method for children with combined sight and hearing problems. Co-active movement employs gross motor activities to structure interaction. The activities are sequenced to develop sensorimotor abilities. Co-active programs are individually tailored to the level of the children and include movement activities, such as crawling, walking, jumping, and running, and perceptual activities, such as matching and sorting objects. For example, if the only movement the child makes is to rock, then the teacher begins the program by rocking together with the child.

The first movements are trunk movements performed on the floor without the need of equipment. Trunk movements include rolling, crawling, scooting, swaying, jumping, and hopping. Movements of the arms may be added later (Robinson, 1975). A simple sequence may include creeping or crawling, pulling oneself up on an object, turning around and sitting down, and then repeating the activity. The co-active sequence takes place daily in a particular location. The teacher begins each session by imitating the child's movements. Van Dijk refers to this aspect as "resonance" (Robinson, 1975).

The purpose of resonance is to focus students' attention on the actions of their own bodies. Van Dijk believes that by imitating the movements of the child, awareness of sequence and anticipation are developed. As soon as children show they can anticipate an entire sequence, new physical movements and objects are introduced into the movement sequence. For example, if the co-active movement is to roll on the floor, a pillow may be included in the rolling activity, thereby turning the child's attention to something concrete in the environment.

When sequences of gross motor movements are well established, Van Dijk advises the omission of parts of sequences to see if there is recognition that parts are missing. At this stage in the sequence, any sign or signal that children produce to indicate their awareness of "something missing" is immediately reinforced (Robinson, 1975). Auditory training, visual training, imitation, and fine motor development in preparation for language training are gradually incorporated into program goals.

The goals of co-active movement include:

1. Establishment of relationship between child and teacher
2. Awareness of sensation
3. Sensory integration
4. Gross motor skills
5. Object manipulation
6. Language and communication

Co-active movement programs are particularly suitable for nonverbal (noncommunicating) children who have some vision and some degree of control over their physical movements.

Development of the Hand

Discussion of hand development is included in this chapter because of its importance in the achievement of mastery skills. Tactile exploration is the only means available to blind children to achieve intimate and direct contact with the physical world. Their interests, curiosity, and interaction with the environment are expressed through the actions of their hands. Hand and intellect are inseparably connected; busy hands express busy minds (Kellogg, 1963).

Manual dexterity depends upon the organization and coordination of finger movements. The fine adjustments made between fingers and palm permit high levels of manual dexterity (Elliott & Connolly, 1984). Benton (1979a) observed a close relationship between the efficient tactile exploration and skilled motor planning. The hands work as a team, with the dominant hand taking the lead and the nondominant hand helping. Controlled bimanual coordination is necessary for fine manipulations (Williams, 1983).

Manual strength and dexterity develop in a progression from birth. The infant's hands are active at birth, able to produce the reflexive grasp that is stimulated by placing an object in the infant's palm (Twitchell, 1970). Voluntary grasping replaces the reflexive grasp at the same time that the flexion of the fingers appears. New patterns of coordinated movements emerge after infants are able to support their weight on their arms and hands.

Grasp is further refined with the articulation of the fingers and the rotation of the thumb. Thumb-finger opposition, a uniquely human characteristic, gives the hand its power. Adequate contact and manipulation of potentially interesting objects refine the infant's ability to grasp and handle objects. Trevarthen (1979) observed that vision and touch work together to produce the complicated reaching/grasping movements of the 3-month-old infant. Infants use their vision to guide the handling of objects by the age of 40 weeks. At this age infants are actively using their hands to reach, touch, and hold a variety of objects (Williams, 1983).

Prehension is the holding and grasping of objects (Napier, 1976). Nonprehensile movements include the movements of the fingers involved in typewriting, piano playing, or reading braille, as well as pushing and lifting movements. Prehension is characterized by two main grips, the power grip and the precision grip. The power grip requires the strength of the whole hand, while precision grips are executed between the fleshy pad of the opposed thumb and the pads of the fingertips. There is, however, an element of precision in the power

Laura, age 6, learning hand manipulation

grip, just as there is an element of power in the precision grip. Precision grips permit the handling and use of small objects, such as needles, pens, and paintbrushes. Aside from the main grips, there are two subsidiary grips: the hook grip and the scissor grip. The hook grip is used for carrying objects, and the scissor grip is used to pick up small objects.

The high level of sensorimotor organization of the hands is reflected in the coordination of type of grip with size and shape of object to be grasped. Learning how to apply the grips comes with repeated experiences with different types of objects (Napier, 1976). Conscious awareness of hand movements is always involved in fine manipulations, such as using a tool or playing a piano (Tubiana, Thomine, & Mackin, 1984).

Finger Dexterity

Most kinds of dexterous movements involve coordinated patterns of finger movement, particularly multiple coordinations between fingers and thumb. Whether the movements are rotary or linear, they involve the fingers in a coordinated sequence. For example, in order to twirl a pencil between the fingers, the fingers are required to change their position while supporting the pencil. Elliott and Connolly (1984) classified the hand movements associated with dexterity into three categories: (1) simple synergies, (2) reciprocal synergies, and (3) sequential patterns.

Simple synergies only require one movement as in pinching or squeezing; the fingers and thumb are maintained in one position. In simple synergies all the movements of the fingers are the same—that is, all the fingers are bent or all are extended. There may be alternate flexing and extending, such as repeatedly squeezing a rubber ball (see Figure 4.1).

In contrast to simple synergies, reciprocal synergies require alternating thumb and finger movements, such as bending the thumb when the fingers extend, and bending the fingers when the thumb is extended. A high proportion of movements fall into this category, such as rolling a small object between the thumb and fingers of the hand (see Figure 4.2).

Sequential patterns use the same movements as other patterns but in a coordinated sequence. Sequential patterns are involved in changing the position of the fingers to shift the position of the object (see Figure 4.3).

Developing Hand Function

The importance of hand development in relation to object knowledge is obvious. When children do not actively use their hands to explore and manipulate, they do not develop concepts about the things in the environment; they remain ignorant of forms, textures, and uses. Failure to develop manual skills is typical of children who do not interact with the environment. Limp and lifeless hands are expressions of a total lack of interest and involvement.

A recent study (Rogow, 1987) investigated object manipulation and manual dexterity among 148 blind, visually impaired, and visually impaired multiply handicapped children. There were three significant findings in this study:

1. A significant relationship was shown between object manipulation and language ability.
2. Automatisms such as dominance and the ability to grasp are not sufficient conditions for the development of object manipulation.
3. There is an inverse relationship between object manipulation and

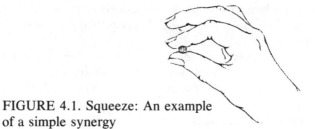

FIGURE 4.1. Squeeze: An example
of a simple synergy

FIGURE 4.2. Twiddle: An example
of a reciprocal synergy

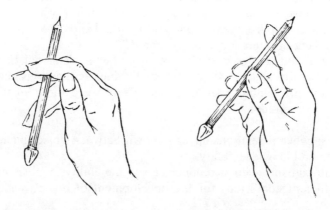

FIGURE 4.3. Digital step: An example of a sequential pattern

atypical or stereotypic hand mannerisms, which are seemingly purposeless manual activities such as hand flapping, mouthing of fingers, finger twitching and finger waving in front of the eyes.

Children with sensory integrative disorders may show adverse responses to tactile stimuli. This condition, in which the child is resistant to using his or her hands, is sometimes referred to as "tactile defensiveness." Visually impaired children who neglect their hands probably have not developed an inner image of their hands and need to discover them. Fortunately, children's hands can be coaxed back to life, as can those of older individuals.

Sacks (1985) described the hand development of a totally blind woman, whom he called Madeline J., who had cerebral palsy. Her hands were only mildly spastic and her sensory capacities seemed to be intact. She could identify light touch, pain, and temperature, but was unable to recognize or identify anything by touch. "She could not identify—and she did not explore; there were no active 'interrogatory' movements of her hands—they were, indeed, as inactive, as inert, as useless, as 'lumps of dough'" (Sacks, 1985, p. 57).

Sacks (1985) wondered if never having used one's hands could account for their "uselessness" and referred to the work of two Russian physicians, Leont'ev and Zaporozhets, who wrote about the "alienation" from their hands experienced by patients whose hands had been injured. In contrast to the injured, Madeline, like the children described in this chapter, had not discovered her hands. In order to get Madeline to begin to use her hands, items of food were left on a tray close to her, but far enough away so she had to reach for them. She was told where the food was located. As Madeline began to discover her hands, she became interested in using them. She found in clay a medium of artistic expression and became an accomplished sculptor. While not everyone may turn out to be as talented as Madeline, the light of discovery nevertheless shines in the faces of all children who begin to use their hands.

The progress made by Mimi illustrates the benefits of developing hand function in children with severe physical handicaps. Seven-year-old Mimi is both visually impaired and physically handicapped. She appeared to be normal at birth, but at 3 months developed a form of epilepsy known as infantile spasms. Medication has not been completely effective in the control of her seizures. She continues to have frequent, brief episodes of a variety of seizure types: head drops, myoclonic seizures, and tremors.

Hand-over-hand techniques were used to show Mimi how to use her hands. No motion was neglected; pushing, pulling, poking, holding, and rolling were included. Even though Mimi is unable to control or rotate her wrist without assistance, she was encouraged to experience a variety of tactile activities such as finger-painting, working with Play-Doh, and holding, rolling, pushing, and pulling a variety of objects. The first goal was to help Mimi become aware of her hands. The second goal was to develop manual strength. Tearing tissue paper, finger painting, squeezing rubber balls, Play-Doh, and plasticine provided a variety of forms of sensory feedback. These activities focused Mimi's attention on her hands.

As awareness developed, Mimi improved her ability to locate objects. As soon as she could locate objects on her tray, a switch was introduced and Mimi learned to push the switch to turn on a radio. This gave her experience with control over the environment. A small electronic organ also helped Mimi to become aware of the movements of her hands and fingers. This instrument gave Mimi additional feedback and enabled her to see the connection between the use of her hands and a desired outcome.

Interestingly, as Mimi began to experience awareness of her hands, she developed more visual control. As she began to "look" at her hands and other objects, drawing and "writing" were introduced. Her teacher supported Mimi's hand with her own, and showed her how to form circles and squares. In a short time she was able to form these shapes on her own. Mimi remembered the shapes and knew them by name. Letters were then introduced and Mimi learned them as well. Writing has become a means of communication. With physical support to her hand, Mimi is writing words and phrases and is able to indicate how much knowledge she had absorbed but was unable to express. When writing, Mimi's attention is focused and her actions are deliberate.

Manual activities focus attention on the actions of the hand and create awareness of what hands "can do." Developing manual ability includes strengthening the hand, developing bimanual coordination, and teaching exploration and manipulation with a variety of plastic and hard materials. Clay, paints, crayons, blocks, balls, and paper can be used to provide a variety of sensory as well as motor experiences.

Summary

Sensorimotor learning is the basis of mastery skills such as object recognition and manipulation, locomotion, concept development, and other forms of independent action within the environment. Connor,

Mimi's drawing of circles and squares

Williamson, and Siepp (1978) noted that motor development cannot be seen as separate from sensory development—hence the term *sensorimotor* development. Normal developmental milestones, such as sitting, standing, and walking alone, may not be achieved by children with severe movement disorders. Sensorimotor learning can be inhibited by physical handicaps that delay the development of normal postural responses. Movement disorders, however mild, can interfere with achievement of postural responses such as equilibrium and inhibit motor learning. Bobath (1985) noted that equilibrium responses are only present in children who can crawl in a fairly normal manner and who can sit alone and use their hands.

Abnormal movement patterns, regularly observed in severely spastic children, can also be observed in children with moderate or slight spasticity (Bobath, 1985). Primitive reflexes, described in Chapter 2, persist when the higher centers of the brain have not absorbed the functions of primitive reflexes. Nonetheless, visually impaired children with motor limitations can be helped to realize a body self with stimulation of the vestibular and proprioceptive senses.

The active self is the connecting link between inner perceptions and external events. This chapter has been concerned with the emergence of the self, including the body self, and the reciprocal interdependence between body image and sensorimotor learning. Learning in the sensorimotor domain demands the active involvement of the learner.

5.

Language and Communication

The ability of children to make sense of their environments and interpret events also makes it possible for them to learn language (M. Donaldson, 1978). It is precisely because the meanings of things and actions are understood that the meaning of language can be discerned. Meaning is discovered in the course of social and environmental interactions, and through these interactions children become competent communicators and users of language. In Chapters 1 and 2, the nature of communication in infancy was introduced. The present chapter deals in greater detail with the development of communication and language. The topics to be addressed include the contributions of language research, language disorders, strategies of teaching communication and language, and augmentative communication for nonspeaking children.

Noncommunicating children become intensely frustrated and deeply fearful of a world they do not understand and feel unable to influence. Along with self-awareness and sensorimotor learning, communication and language are foundations of learning. Communication is the heart of social interaction and must be given a high priority in educational intervention. Part of teaching children to communicate is teaching them the "how" as well as the "what" of communication and language. This means teaching children how to learn as well as what to learn. Communication comes first, before vocabulary or grammar.

Language, so deeply a part of human existence, is complex and multifaceted. The following definitions clarify the terms associated with language development in children.

Communication: Social interactions in which information is exchanged between two or more individuals.
Language: Highly organized symbolized systems. The symbols may be sound symbols (spoken words), written symbols, or manual signs.
Receptive language: Comprehension of oral, written, or manual language symbols.

Expressive language: Production of speech, manual signs, or other symbol system.

Language behaviors: Symbolic behaviors directed toward another person(s).

Semantics: The meaning of words, phrases, and sentences.

Phonology: The particular sounds and arrangement of sounds utilized by spoken languages.

Syntax: The grammar of language, governed by implicit rules concerning the structure of phrases and sentences.

Speech: The ability to articulate and voice the sounds of oral language.

Pragmatics: The social functions of language, e.g., speaking to get something, to tell something, or to ask for something.

Communicative competence: The ability to receive, interpret, and produce messages to communicate with other people.

The communicative functions of language depend a great deal on the speaker's knowledge of the environment. As M. Donaldson (1978) observed, it is the ability to make sense of situations that makes it possible to learn language. Communicative competence entails encoding and decoding messages and learning how to use these messages to perform communicative functions (McLean & Snyder-McLean, 1984). Communication occurs when both the speaker and the listener understand the same meaning. The functions of communication include such intents as (McLean & Snyder-McLean, 1984):

Regulating listener's attention to self or to an item of interest
Regulating listener's actions
Giving and getting information
Indicating desire for interaction
Describing and interpreting events
Learning a new behavior

Communicative competence consists of being able to perform the full array of language functions. Children who are in communication with the people around them are able to effectively influence the events of their lives.

Contributions of Language Research

Developmental linguistics has solved some of the mystery of how very young children acquire their native language. As Bruner (1983) noted, language is not encountered "willy nilly." Language research reveals the intricate interdependence of language with all aspects of human interactions.

The Physiological Basis of Language and Speech

Speech and language, like other complex human behaviors have their roots in physiology. Language learning begins with the ability to hear language. As Mysak (1980) has pointed out, efficient hearing for speech requires trunk and head balance and the ability to localize sound. Well-organized listening responses are illustrated by the ability to localize sound and perceive speech. The nerve pathways serving speech and language grow rapidly in the first year. These nerve pathways are stimulated by the quality and quantity of stimuli received from the environment; several important centers in the brain have the specific function of receiving and organizing language information for interpretation and output.

A high level of sensory integration is involved in speech production. The sensory receptors involved in speech include the ear, the eye, and the tactile receptors. The ear receives sound pressure energy associated with speech events. The eye receives information about articulatory movements, as well as facial and bodily expressions associated with speech events. The lips, tongue, fingertips, palm, soft palate, and areas of the thorax receive the tactile-kinesthetic sensations associated with speech (Mysak, 1976). The integration of the speech receptors makes it possible to hear a speech signal, attend to it, interpret it, and produce it. As speech information is being conveyed, the mechanisms of integration "turn on," "tune in," and "fine tune" the speech system. Integration of the motor mechanisms of speech coordinates breathing and voicing with the articulatory movements of lips and tongue (Mysak, 1976), Skilled speech movements represent "the integration and elaboration of all subcortical mechanisms involved in speech functions" (Mysak, 1980, p. 94).

Lenneberg (1967) maintained that the sequential development of oral language was linked to the maturation of other physical functions such as gait and motor coordination. He proposed the notion of a "critical" period of language learning from about age 2 to age 13. During this period language is acquired far more easily than it is after puberty. It is widely recognized that profoundly deaf children have a better chance of developing speech if amplification and training begin as close to the age of 2 years as possible (Lenneberg, 1967).

The stages of speech and language reflect the progressive integration and elaboration of physiological functions such as hearing, breathing, hand function, and mouth movements (Mysak, 1980). Mysak's view is based on neuroevolutionary theory, discussed in the previous chapter. Mysak (1980) offered a model of the emergence of coordinated speech that is based on the progressive coordination and integration of body postures, arm and hand movements, facial expressions, and vocalization leading to the development of speech. There are four successive, overlapping stages; each stage incorporates the accomplishments of the preceding stages. Mysak refers to the four stages as Body Talk, Hands Talk, Face Talk, and Mouth Talk.

Body Talk is the first stage and is generally characteristic of infants through the age of 6 months. This stage begins at birth with relatively generalized and undifferentiated vocalizations and movements of the body and hands and continues as progressively more complex and differentiated expressiveness emerges. The infant's first sounds are cries and gurgles. At about the age of 5 months, the infant's attention begins to shift from the contours of speech to individual segments of speech sounds (consonants, vowels, and diphthongs). At the end of the stage of body talk, infants' babbling begins to conform to the sound patterns of their parents' language. Entry into the stage of hands talk is marked by the discovery that when lips and tongues are moved in certain ways, the same sounds can be produced over and over again.

Hands Talk serves as a form of symbolic communication. For example, hands outstretched to signal "pick me up," shaking the head to indicate "I don't want it," opening the hand and reaching to mean "give it to me." Later on, hands talk accompanies and facilitates speech. At this stage, beginning at about age 4 months, motoric and vocal expressions convey a variety of meanings.

Face Talk begins with infants' interest in facial expressions, signaling happiness, sadness, being excited, and so forth. This period occurs during the second six months of life (Mysak, 1980). During this stage, there is the emergence of a wide variety of facial expressions used for communication. Babies at this stage produce a variety of vocalizations, including imitations of animal sounds and other environmental noises. The expressions of the hands, body, and face are coordinated with vocal behavior. Crying, cooing, babbling, lalling, and echoing are forms of preverbal vocalization.

Mouth Talk begins with the onset of true articulated speech. With control of the tongue and lips and the growth of teeth to provide a frontal wall for the oral cavity, cortical control of speech sounds begins. Infants voluntarily imitate the speech of others as well as their own speech sounds (Mysak, 1980). As children become skillful in producing speech sounds, they learn to associate certain sounds with the people, objects, and events of their environments. The ability to talk depends upon the coordination and integration of receptive and expressive mechanisms of speech and language (Mysak, 1980). True words appear after the motor system for speech has been coordinated with breath control and movements of the lips and tongue. Perception, comprehension, and formulation of speech depend upon memory, retrieval, and response functions.

The Social Basis of Speech and Language

There is broad agreement among language scientists that the roots of competent language performance reside in social interaction. As DeLaguna (1927/1963) pointed out, "Men do speak not simply to relieve their feelings or to air their views, but to awaken a response in their fellows and to influence their attitudes and acts" (p. 20). Verbal language is only one part of communication (Von Raffler-Engel, 1981). The data derived from research on emerging speech indicate that communicative efficiency is established long before children are able to speak (Bates, 1979). Before children speak, they become artful in the expression of intention. Even after language is acquired, many aspects of grammatical form and content are shaped by the social nature of language function (McLean & Snyder-McLean, 1984).

The Beginnings of Communication: Intentionality

Intentionality becomes apparent when a consistent signal is associated with a specific outcome (Bates, 1979). Children begin to express intention as soon as they become aware of the effects of their actions (signals) on other people. For example, holding out an empty glass to be filled comes to mean "Please fill this glass" or "I want a drink" or "more." These signals are signs related to referents. Holding the glass towards the adult is a sign, referring to the desired drink. Signs are social signals.

Bates (1979) noted that the use of conventional signals is the first step toward symbolic representation and language. The shift from social signals toward conventional linguistic signs, a prerequisite for language, is based on the recognition that sounds and gestures function to communicate. The form and function of sounds and gestures take on meanings that are shared by parent and child (Bates, 1979). Between the ages of 9 and 15 months, children are using a range of vocal and gestural signals that function to get and keep attention, greet and request. The first conventional vocal signs are protowords, intended to represent persons, places, events, and objects. Protowords function as words.

Greenfield and Smith (1976) defined three functional categories of children's earliest communicative vocalizations. The first is the performative category in which vocalizations accompany actions. Vocalizations may include onomatopoeic sounds like "grrr" and "whoosh." The second category is indicative. These vocalizations call attention to objects and are often accompanied by looking or pointing. The third category is made up of "demand" sounds that function as request signals. Bullowa (1979) noted that at first, vocalizations accompany hand gestures for both indicative and demand functions, and that hand gestures are later replaced with words. Single-word speech is closely tied to overt actions; for example, "jump, jump, jump," the first words articulated by one child, were said as she was jumping.

Watson (1972) explored the adult's role in the development of social signals. Adults play the babies' game by providing their infants with contingency experiences. For example, if the adult imitates the child after the infant coos, the infant learns to coo in order to receive the adult's response. Very young children learn to anticipate adult responses and act in order to elicit them. Goldberg (1977) observed that the more "readable" the child's signal, the more consistent the adult response.

Mutual responding leads to a synchronized meshing of the actions of child and adult, creating intimate and intense moments of shared pleasure (Trevarthen, 1980). Halliday (1975) proposed that reciprocal vocal responding is preparation for vocalizing "acts of meaning."

The earliest language patterns perceived by infants are the sound contours of language. These are patterns of pitch, tone, and stress (Stern, 1977). Adults help children learn by exaggerating the contours. They raise and lower their voices, prolong syllables, and slow down the rate of speech. These exaggerations draw the infant's attention to the sound contours. Listening to speech is closely tied to feelings of emotional well-being; infants hear speech when they are being held, cuddled, or otherwise given adult attention.

Development of Syntax and Vocabulary

In order to communicate with language, there must be both a vocabulary and a grammar. The words of a language are its smallest units of meaning. The organization of words into sentences is governed by "rules"; this is the grammar of language. Every language has its own prescribed and implicit rules for the ordering of words into sentences. The English language depends a great deal on word order for conveying the meanings of sentences. The "actor" is distinguished from the "acted upon" by the sequence of words in an utterance, as can be seen by comparing the sentences, "The man saved the dog" and "The dog saved the man." How children construct their own notions of the meanings and rules of language is revealed by the stages of language development.

The one-word comments of beginning speech derive most of their meanings from the context in which they are spoken (deVilliers & deVilliers, 1978). One-word comments are spoken with knowledge of intent; they are used as statements, demands, or questions. The ways in which adults respond to children's comments provide the structures for learning more about what language can accomplish. Consider the following conversation between a child and her mother.

Child: (pointing to a glass on the table) Mik? [milk]
Mother: No, that's your apple juice.
Child: Appeju?
Mother: Yes, apple juice.

The question is marked by a rise of the voice, and it quickly elicits a response from the child's mother. This sort of question is a contingent query and brings the child immediate feedback on the intelligibility of her question. Contingent queries are strategies for learning language (Garvey, 1977b). The unsolicited query also helps the child to influence the stream of conversation.

Knowledge of the relationships between persons, objects, and events precedes the ability to encode these relationships in language (Bloom, 1973; Brown, 1973; Bruner, 1975; deVilliers & deVilliers, 1978; Garvey, 1977b). Vocabularies are expanded as children build categories of objects and events. Most importantly, young children become adept at interpreting the language of others and entering into conversations with other people (deVilliers & deVilliers, 1978).

The fact that words co-occur with nonlinguistic events provides rich clues to their meaning (M. Donaldson, 1978). Words are learned as categories of experience. Vocabularies are not built one word at a time, nor is the full meaning of words acquired all at once (Crystal, 1976). Words representing persons, actions, places, and things appear to be acquired before pronouns, adjectives, or adverbs. Young children tackle the meanings of words with two strategies; overextension and overrestriction. For example, one small child refers to every event she wishes to terminate as "Awduh" (All done). "All done" also means "I'm finished" and "Hurry up."

Attaching meaning to words is a process that requires both abstraction and generalization, for a one-to-one correspondence between word and referent only exists in the case of proper nouns. Indeed, words that refer to feelings or intangible things, as well as those that signal intention, desire, or need, have no counterpart at all in the real world. Other strategies, such as contrasting word pairs, must be utilized. For example, Chukovsky, in his classic study (1968), noted that children are fascinated by opposites and thus learn the meaning of *big* along with the meaning of *little*.

The order of acquisition of specific linguistic forms suggests how important the child's recognition of underlying semantic intention is to language comprehension (Bloom, 1973). The question form appears early; children are experienced processors of questions before the age of 3 years (Brown, 1973). Between the ages of 2 and 3, children become full-fledged speakers and use their language in an array of purposive ways. They declare, command, inquire, request, pretend, and enter into conversation with adults. Knowledge of language functions keeps apace with knowledge of language forms. By the time they are 4 years old, most children have mastered the basic rules of syntax, have extensive vocabularies, and use language in imaginative and social ways.

Young children take language seriously, which is probably why nonsense rhymes and statements are so appealing to them. The statement "Brush your teeth with your comb" is funny only when incongruity is recognized. Awareness of the real order of things lies behind enjoyment of nonsense. The more aware the child is, the more comical is the violation of the order of things (Chukovsky, 1976).

Children learning language appear to give special attention to the ordering of words within an utterance. They learn the simplest and most obvious principles before the more complex (Brown, 1973). Syntax is derived from the meaning the child intends to convey. Consider the phrases, "Daddy shoe," "Mommy go," "drink milk." Each demonstrates discernment of a semantic relationship (Bloom, 1973). According to deVilliers and deVilliers (1978) the earliest semantic relations expressed are the following:

Agent and action: "Boy cries," "Daddy goes."
Action and object: "Want more," "See shoe."
Agent and object: "Mommy cake" [Mommy is eating cake].
Negation: "No wash" [I do not want to be washed].
Action and locative: "Sit chair" [Sit in the chair].
Entity and locative: "Cup shelf" [The cup is on the shelf].
Possessor and possessed: "Mommy hat" [Mommy's hat].
Entity and attribute: "Ball red" [The ball is red].
Demonstrative and entity: "There car" [There is a car].

The use of words such as articles, adjectives, adverbs, pronouns, prepositions, and auxiliary verbs emerges together with the development of noun and verb phrases. The basic grammatical rules are learned as the understanding of language functions increases.

Pragmatics, or the social functions of language, are essential to language mastery. What children seem to know most about language is how it works for them. Language development reflects cognitive growth, but cognitive growth is also dependent on language development. Whether language should be considered as part of the domain of cognitive development or as a domain in its own right is a moot point. Language enriches the meaning of experience and contributes to understanding the real world. Because language is unique in its communicative functions, even its rudimentary presence can make a big difference; it is possible to become a good communicator while commanding only a very limited vocabulary and only a few rules.

At the beginning levels of building communicative competence, emotional well-being cannot be separated from cognitive processes. Increased communication is the best indicator of progress.

Language Intervention

As noted in Chapter 3, the language development of visually impaired children does not differ in significant ways from that of the sighted, unless there is some interference or delay in normal social interactions. Problems do arise, however, when there is too little interaction. Bruner (1975) suggested that language is acquired in the service of communicative functions. Studies of the emergence of prelinguistic communication suggest that intervention programs may need to be directed at gestural or even more primitive levels of communication with children who have severe communicative deficits (McLean & Snyder-McLean, 1984). The first level of remediation is the development of communicative responses. The goals of communication programming for noncommunicating children include:

Establishment of communicative responses
Awareness of signs and symbols
Imitation
Consistent use of social signals

Noncommunicating Children

The inarticulate, inexpressible loneliness of children who do not know how to reach out to other people, who know nothing of sharing intimate moments, was well expressed by Helen Keller in an autobiographical account. Calling herself "Phantom," she wrote:

> Phantom did not seek a solution for her chaos because she knew not what it was. Nor did she seek death because she had no conception of it. All she touched was a blur without wonder or anticipation, curiosity or conscience. (Keller, 1955, p. 26)

Research evidence demonstrating a continuity between early communicative performances and later language performances has provided a strong basis for targeting nonlinguistic communicative behaviors as the first aim of intervention for noncommunicating children (McLean & Snyder-McLean, 1984). Such intervention requires identifying a means by which the three essential elements of communication—a mode of communication—can be developed in the child. Prelanguage communication, which consists of interaction in which a message is conveyed, may take a variety of forms: touching a person or object, assisting an adult, showing an object, pointing to an object, gesturing, or vocalizing. At least some of these communicative behaviors must be displayed before formal language instruction, utilizing signs, speech, or other abstract symbols, can begin.

Developing Communicative Responses and Social Signals

Beginning communication with nonresponsive children requires a social context for interaction. In this section, an approach using social routines based on nursery rhymes is described as an effective method of establishing shared attention, mutual responding, and social signals in noncommunicating children. The goal is to develop communicative responses such as gestures, postural movements, or vocalizations that indicate participation, enjoyment, or a request to continue or end the interaction. Nursery rhymes paired with action sequences provide the structure for adult-child interaction. The advantage of using nursery rhymes is that the chants are rhythmic, easily recognizable, and full of action. They lend themselves to physical movement. When paired with action sequences, the rhymes become social routines.

Social routines are structured interactions that have well-defined beginnings and endings. The structure of the routines focuses the child's attention on the actions of the adult. As Bruner (1975) noted, social games or routines encourage attention to the behavior of the partner and lead to shared attention and reciprocal actions. Nursery rhyme routines create a context for reciprocity of action and an awareness of the role of adult partner. The goals of social routines are:

Attention to and participation in a shared event
Imitation of adult vocal or gestural behavior
Coordination of actions and joint reference (shared attention)
Self-regulated response to adult requests
Spontaneous, purposive actions

A program based on nursery rhymes paired with action sequences was developed to establish communicative responses in noncommunicative children. Traditional nursery rhymes were chosen because of their familiarity, their poetry and rhythm, and the ease of combining them with motor actions. Each nursery rhyme was paired with its own sequence. For example, the rhyme "London Bridge" was combined with holding the child's hands and swaying back and forth. "Humpty Dumpty," "Old King Cole," and "Jack Be Nimble" were each combined with a different sequence of actions. The words of these rhymes are full of action and lend themselves to rhythmic chanting.

Vocalization, body posture, and hand gestures were treated as social signals. For example, one child began vocalizing as soon as she heard the voice of the adult. These vocalizations were acknowledged and treated as an invitation to play. Another child approached her teacher with her arms outstretched to signal readiness for play. The rhythmic sequences assisted the children to remember the rhymes and coordinate their actions with those of the adults. Children responded in the modality in which they were the least restricted: The more physically handicapped children used vocalization, while the physically active used body position and gesture (Rogow, 1982).

Random vocalizations, hand movements, or body postures are transformed into effective social signals when adults respond consistently. The rhythm of the chants helps to direct children's attention to the sounds. In order to match actions to the rhymes, children must listen. Through social routines, noncommunicating children discover that they can influence and participate in interactions.

Social routines were also created to teach specific actions. Amanda, a developmentally delayed totally blind child, was not walking independently. To encourage Amanda to walk alone we developed a routine with the chant:

Amanda is trailing the wall,
She is trailing the wall in the hall

After being shown how to trail the wall, Amanda placed her arm on the wall and began walking independently. She no longer needed a social routine as a prompt to respond to the request.

Imitation

Imitation is both a form of communication and a strategy of learning. Children imitate only after they become aware of another person and choose to "be like" that person. Imitation for children with severe visual impairments may not occur until after language is comprehended. Vision facilitates the use of imitation as a learning strategy. Lack of clear vision delays the development of imitation.

The case of 3-year-old Laura, who has congenital bilateral cataracts and Down's syndrome, illustrates the value of imitation as a learning strategy. Laura used a variety of social signals to initiate play with an adult. She extended her arms for "London Bridge" and took hold of the adult's hands to play "Patty Cake." When Laura was fitted with contact lenses, she was able to establish eye contact and began to study both her mother's face and her teacher's. Laura enjoyed watching her teacher make "funny faces" and began to imitate. Her teacher quickly noticed this new behavior and sought to expand on it: "Laura watches my face intently. I made different faces, sticking out my tongue, blowing air with a 'brrr' sound, frowning, and grinning. Laura's eyes never left my face. After a few minutes of watching me, Laura tried to mimic the 'brrr' and stuck her tongue out."

Before long, Laura began inventing her own imitation games, making a face or holding her arm up in the air and then waiting for the teacher to imitate her. On one occasion, her teacher did not respond immediately and waited to see what Laura would do. Laura held up her arm and looked at her teacher. Then she repeated the motion.

When the teacher still did not respond, Laura took the teacher's arm and held it up.

Not all children use imitation as a learning strategy, as Laura did. Amanda, for example, did not begin to imitate until she started to talk. Her first word was a communicative imitation. Her teacher noted: "When I was leaving with my coat on she sure didn't want me to go. She kept grabbing my coat making a whole bunch of sounds. Finally I had to go so I said, 'Yes, yes, yes,' and she repeated 'Yes' as loud and clear as a bell."

It is interesting to note, however, that in both Amanda's case and Laura's, first words either were pure imitations or were embedded in the actions in which the child was engaged; in other words, both children used language in conjunction with action.

It is easier for children to give signals and gain pleasure from adults' responses than to respond to adults' signals. Choose activities that children enjoy and treat their actions as if they were signals. As soon as one signal is being used consistently, interpret other gestures as signals. Teach signals by modeling them. Speech should be used in conjunction with gestures so that associations are built between gesture signals and words. Play games using the signals and provide immediate response. With children who have hearing as well as visual impairments, sharp, clearly defined gestures, such as clapping or patting the body, are easiest to develop. Van Dijk developed gestures for objects by noting the actions used with the objects and then emphasizing them—for example, a brushing motion on the teeth to represent a toothbrush.

Communicative signals serve a variety of purposes. Among these are:

Request object/action: A behavior directed toward obtaining something.

Request attention: An action directed toward getting an adult's attention.

Protest: Actions indicating "No, I don't want to."

Social: Greetings such as "Hi" or "Bye."

Comment: Pointing at or otherwise indicating something about an object, such as "That's mine."

Permission/question: Actions such as a shrug of the shoulders or looking around for an object that may indicate either "Where is the ball?" or "Can I?"

Offer: An action, such as extending an object, that indicates an intention to give something to another person.

Pictorial Symbols

Vision plays an important role in communication. Some visually impaired children have enough sight to see pictures that can be used as a symbol system. The visual modality may be the mode of choice for children who are not physically adept or mobile.

Janice has both vision and hearing handicaps related to rubella. When she was 8 years old, Janice had extreme behavior problems. In school, her screaming and frequent tantrums were making it impossible to contain her in a classroom setting. She upset the other children and demanded constant attention. A meeting was held with Janice's mother to determine a strategy that could be used both at home and at school. During the interview, the teachers learned that Janice enjoyed looking at pictures of food in the newspapers. Her mother reported that every evening Janice searched the paper and tore out advertisements showing pictures of food. This gave the teachers an idea about how to communicate with Janice. Simple signs were made by pasting clearly identifiable pictures of a variety of common objects—a cookie, a glass, a child's coat, a bed, and a sink on individual plastic chips. Janice was given a small straw basket to hold the chips. Her teacher gave her a chip to introduce an activity or to make a request. At snack time, Janice requested a cookie by giving the appropriate chip to her teacher. With her new ability to communicate, Janice's behavior improved and she became more willing to participate in activities with other children.

Speech and Language Disorders

Language refines, shapes, and extends the power of communication. Some children become efficient communicators even in the absence of language. They gesture or take the adults' hands and physically take them to objects or activities they desire, but are unable to advance from gesture to symbol. Communication and language development mirrors the quality and quantity of social interaction. Delayed or disordered speech is associated with hearing impairments, mental retardation, perceptual dysfunctions, sensory deprivation, and emotional problems.

Damage to the nerve pathways serving speech and language functions, whether caused by disease, such as encephalitis, or by head trauma, may result in the loss of linguistic ability. Such injury can occur before, during, or after birth, and the age of onset of brain damage is a critical factor in recovery. In children under 3, recovery may be complete. After the age of 3, recovery is likely to be slower and some residual problems may remain (Leonard, 1982). There is evidence that language functions can be assumed by other areas of the brain if injury occurs early enough. Linguistic ability may be regained if the damage occurs before the age of 9 and is confined to only one hemisphere of the brain (Lenneberg, 1967).

Language and speech disorders associated with neurological impairments are on a continuum, ranging from disorders of the perception and interpretation of speech (decoding) to the organization and production of speech (encoding). Speech and language disorders in children range from mild language learning difficulties to profoundly debilitating disorders. Inability to communicate effectively with verbal language profoundly affects the social interactions of children. Speech is the primary sensorimotor aspect of language. Problems in understanding language are always reflected in speech, but speech disorders can exist even when there is full comprehension of language. Speech and language disorders are generally classified as receptive, expressive, or a combination of both.

Receptive Language Disorders

Receptive disorders interfere with recognition and comprehension of language (Byrne & Shervanian, 1977). Afflicted persons hear speech and know that they are being spoken to, but they cannot comprehend what is being said. The terms "aphasia" and "dysphasia" describe receptive disorders. Children with aphasia-related problems have difficulty attending to the spoken word. DeVilliers and deVilliers (1978), summing up the research on aphasia in childhood, noted that affected children have problems with rapid sound changes. Inability to process rapid speech impairs the ability of the aphasic child to identify and discriminate consonants. Sometimes receptivity improves when the rate of speech is considerably slowed and one word is spoken at a time in a louder voice. Aphasia affects all aspects of language behavior, hindering comprehension and formulation of grammatic utterances, word usage, and the expression of meaning (Byrne & Shervanian, 1977).

Expressive Disorders

Expressive disorders affect the production of language and interfere with the flow of speech. Language is created out of sound patterns that exist in the dimension of time. Disarranged timing and discoordinations occur when the various organs involved in speaking—the lips, tongue, palate, and vocal chords—fail to interact at the right time. The child is thus unable to motor plan the ordering of the units of speech, which "tumble into the production line uninhibited by higher syntactic principles" (Lenneberg, 1967, p. 219).

Lenneberg compared the composition of discourse to the assembly of a train. An overall plan determines the order of the cars, which are held in readiness until the time they are to be released and hitched onto the moving train; the individual coaches are attached while the locomotive moves ahead. So it is with planning speech: We know what we want to say and we order the words to convey our meaning. To the degree that there is a loss of the capacity to order and plan, words become jumbled and meanings are lost. Fluency becomes impossible. Fluency problems may appear as too much or too little fluency; conditions referred to as subfluency and superfluency, respectively.

Praxis is the ability to perform specific motor movements, such as the movements of the lips and tongue. *Apraxic* speech reflects loss of control over the articulating sequences and results in subfluent speech. Another type of subfluency is caused by *dysarthria,* difficulties with voicing or articulation (Mysak, 1980). Children with varying degrees of neurological impairments such as cerebral palsy may have both types of subfluency problems, that is, simultaneous apraxia and dysarthria.

Superfluency occurs when there is a loss of timing, an inability to inhibit or order the words in an utterance; the speaker is unable to hold on to the order of words. The flow of speech is increased and consists of unorganized, unphrased, unfinished, or improperly begun utterances (Lenneberg, 1967). Children with superfluent speech may also have problems in organizing their thoughts.

Some degree of semantic disturbance is usually associated with language disorders. Word-finding difficulties, for example, are a frequent characteristic of disordered language; the speaker knows the word and recognizes it when another speaker says it, but cannot find it when speaking. The experience is similar to "it's on the tip of my tongue" experiences, except that the problem is exaggerated and occurs with frequency when speech is attempted.

The diagnosis and treatment of language disorders in children demand the team effort of speech pathologists, audiologists, physicians, and educators working together. The services of speech pathologists are essential to assessment and intervention. Even relatively minor hearing handicaps can account for the failure of visually impaired children to develop speech. A thorough analysis of children's vocal behaviors, the sounds they are able to make, and the articulatory difficulties they have is essential to determinations of the type of treatment required. Capabilities for speech may be determined with examination of breath, voice, and articulatory control.

There is considerable evidence that children who are unable to speak or even to produce sound may still advance in receptive language skills. Lenneberg (1967) cautioned that inability to articulate should never lead to the assumption that children are unable to comprehend or work with language systems.

> The theoretical importance of the extreme dissociation between perceptive and productive ability lies in the demonstration that the particular ability which we may properly call "having knowledge of a language" is not identical with speaking. (Lenneberg, 1967, p. 308)

Lenneberg reported the case of a 9-year-old boy who had never babbled or spoken, but who had a complete understanding of English. This child had learned to read and demonstrated his reading ability by matching pictures to words and sentences.

The symptoms that should alert parents and teachers to language disorders include (Mysak, 1980):

Marked reduction of language
Syllable reversals within words
Grammatical confusions
Omitted or mistakenly used function words such as in, on
Meaningless verbalization
Word-finding problems
Near normal comprehension with significant lag in expression
Excessive use of gesture
Verbal perseveration
Echolalia

Most of these symptoms may be observed in normal people following trauma to the speech centers of the brain. Among children with severe visual impairments, echolalia and marked reduction of speech are often reflections of a poverty of social interaction and social relationships. Similarly, when intimate social relationships are not established between caregivers and congenitally blind children, impoverished and eccentric language may result.

Jeanine, for example, appeared to have a severe language disorder. A child with delicate and well-formed features, Jeanine was congenitally blind due to optic atrophy. She refused to speak to other people except with one phrase, "I will not do it." The phrase was articulated and grammatical and revealed a high order of language comprehension. Further evidence of Jeanine's command of language was her ability to respond to requests by either compliance or deliberate refusal.

A breakthrough occurred one day when Jeanine's teacher decided to play a word association game with her; the teacher said "table," and Jeanine responded, "chair." As the game continued, eventually totalling more than thirty associations, Jeanine correctly paired nouns with nouns, adjectives with adjectives, and so forth. When she did not understand a word, she rhymed it. To the word "doctor" Jeanine responded "people who can see with their eyes"; the word "bus" elicited "people ride on buses when they can see with their eyes."

After this breakthrough, Jeanine regularly spoke in class. However, an analysis of some 200 of Jeanine's comments revealed them to be mostly declarative or imperative statements; she rarely asked questions and showed little curiosity about the environment. Jeanine felt herself to be deprived by her blindness. She was the first child of a teenage couple; their second child, born a year later, was sighted. Jeanine's mother was deeply troubled by her blindness and made no demands. Jeanine's behavior problems were intensified and she was placed in the care of a foster family. Jeanine thought she was unable to stay at home because she was blind; in her child's mind, her blindness had come to mean rejection. The depth of these feelings can be seen in Jeanine's first spontaneous story, about a girl named Joan: "Joan was sighted. She is a pretend girl. No, she is blind, she lives nowhere."

Jeanine had used not speaking as a strategy to ward off rejection. Not speaking was a way of controlling other people. Jeanine's foster family was included in planning a program to increase her feelings of security and self-worth. As she progressed, her language skills as well as her true abilities became apparent.

Jeanine was 9 years old before she really began to talk with fluency, although it had been evident that she possessed language. Like other children who feel themselves to be isolated or rejected, she could not experience the gratification of being "in communication" with other people. She shared with Doug (in Chapter 4) an inability to experience herself as part of a social environment.

Doug could also speak in full sentences. He knew the words of songs and poems and recited the commercials he heard on the radio or television. Yet he rarely used words to communicate. His speech was described as echolalic because it consisted of repetitions of the words he heard others use.

Teacher: Let's eat our lunch, Doug.
Doug: Let's eat our lunch.
Teacher: Do you want a sandwich?
Doug: The circus is coming. Yes, the circus is coming.
Teacher: Do you like the circus?
Doug: The circus is coming to town.
Teacher: We'll go to the circus in the spring. Do you want your sandwich?
Doug: (no response)

Doug repeated the statements of other people and asked the same questions over and over again, without regard for a reply. His language was unrelated to immediate events happening around him; he had no idea how to use language as a tool of social negotiation.

Both the meaning and social context of language have to be demonstrated to children like Doug. Conversational skills come with a recognition of a need to respond. In conversation one speaker relates to another. These are dialogue or discourse relationships acquired from firsthand experience in interacting with other people in a variety of situations.

Considerations in Remediation

The elements of remedial programming for children like Jeanine and Doug must consider their needs for communication. In a very real sense, these children have circumvented their need to communicate or adapt; their environments have adapted to them. There is a dynamic to nonparticipation. Routines provide the structure of the day and lack of interaction ensures that they are not challenged by new experiences. In order to engage such children in a dialogue with the world, it is necessary to show them that speech is an effective tool and a gratifying medium of exchange with other people.

Children talk in order to have an effect on other people. As McLean and Snyder-McLean (1984) pointed out, techniques of remediation should model the functions as well as the forms of language. In Chapter 6, the uses of dramatic play are illustrated as a means of developing dialogue and conversation skills. The following suggestions have been included for their contribution to developing language:

1. Enrich the speech environment.
2. Draw attention to the sounds of speech.
3. Make language instruction fun and rewarding.

4. Speak into children's hands and let them feel speech and silence.
5. Provide ample time for children to respond.
6. Reinforce speech efforts.
7. Speak slowly and animatedly in complete but simple sentences.
8. Associate language with experience. Accompany actions with descriptive speech.
9. Encourage activities that require the need to talk. Children need something to talk about. Field trips, outdoor activities planned together with children, provide many opportunities for speech.
10. Give children choices.
11. Establish realistic short-term goals.
12. Chart progress daily

Nonspeaking children discourage speech in the people around them. As a consequence they hear less speech. Even though some children appear unresponsive to speech, good speech directed to the child encourages expectations of responses.

All forms of language play help the child to explore the substance and structure of language (Garvey, 1977a). As children play with the sounds and words of language, they integrate and elaborate their understanding of its forms and content. Repetitive, rhythmic vocalizations associated with pleasurable states in the pre-linguistic child—such as sound games, singing, chanting, rhyming, crooning, popping noises, and tongue clicking—help to focus attention on sound production. Babbling is an early form of language play.

For children who comprehend language, language play, playful chanting of words, prolongation of syllables, nonsense rhymes, and poetry cultivate an interest in listening to language. For example, the speech play of very young children centers on the sounds and rhythms of speech. "Now it's done, un un, done, un, un, un" is a typical chant of a 2-year-old. (Garvey, 1977a, p. 62). Fascination with sounds of speech persist long after vocabulary and syntax are acquired.

Supplemental or Augmentative Language Systems

"Augmentative communication" is a generic term referring to any approach "designed to support, enhance, or augment the communication" of children or adults who are not verbal communicators in all situations (Beukelman, Yorkston, & Dowden, 1985, p. 3). Other terms used synonymously are assistive, alternative, nonvocal, or nonoral communication. Augmentative systems fall roughly into two main categories: aided and unaided. Unaided systems rely on gestural communication. Aided systems require the use of some device, ranging from the use of traditional word boards and books to the sophisticated technology of computer-based electronic communication systems. Computer-based augmentative systems will be discussed in Chapter 8. Augmentative communication does not rule out speech, but provides alternative methods of communication for children who do not or cannot talk. Supplemental systems should be introduced as early as possible when there is the suspicion that the child is unable to speak. These systems often act to stimulate language and verbalization.

Supplementary methods are a means to an end, not ends in themselves. Their purpose is the achievement of communication and independent usage of the system. Children must be supported from the initial introduction of the system to the point of independent communication (Davies, 1984). Supplemental programs should be complete and enable initiation of communication as well as response; they should encourage children to communicate. Children who experience repeated failure are deeply discouraged. The desire to communicate can be "rekindled" by easily learned supplemental systems (Davies, 1984). Portability is an important factor. If at all possible, the chosen system should be transferable from home to school and other social situations so that children can use it wherever they go. The chosen system should be transferable from one school to another so that children do not have to begin all over again with a new system, once again condemning them to silence.

Transitions from one system to another may also be considered should the need arise. Supplemental systems are not mutually exclusive. For example, some children may do their language programs with the aid of a communication board and utilize a sign system for social conversation. There should be a match between a system and the communicative purpose it is designed to serve. If the system is to be used for conversation, then it must possess more capability than a system used only for basic needs. Further, the symbols or signs employed by the system should be interpretable by other people; otherwise the child will have learned a system that can be used with a very limited number of people.

Unaided Systems

Unaided systems range from concrete signs representing particular objects or events to formalized signed languages. Natural gestures may be used as unaided communication with children who have little language comprehension. Signed or gestured languages include American (Ameslan) and British Sign Language and a number of other gesture systems in current use.

Ameslan, or American Sign Language, is the oldest and most well-established sign language used by deaf people in North America. Employing manual signs representing words and finger spelling, it is a direct and nonassisted means of communication; however, it is dependent on adequate manual control and visual/kinesthetic retention of signs. Ameslan has its own grammar.

Paget-Gorman Sign System is a conceptually based manual sign system developed in Britain. Its original purpose was to improve the linguistic abilities of deaf children. It has proven useful for other language-impaired children because it allows for a precise interpretation of the spoken word (Davies, 1984).

Amerind, an ancient gestural code system developed by nomadic American Indians, employs easily recognized pantomimic gestures. This system is being successfully employed in Britain and the United States with mentally retarded children (Davies, 1984).

Makaton vocabulary, developed in Great Britain for mentally handicapped people, is a developmental language program using British sign language.

For severely visually impaired children, gesture systems that depend on vision are obviously not suitable. The motoric complexities of gesture systems must also be considered in choosing a gestural supplemental system (Beukelman, Yorkston, & Dowden, 1985).

Aided Systems

Aided systems, which depend on pictographic representations, include Blissymbolics communications and picture boards.

Blissymbolics communication uses pictographic, ideographic, and abstract symbols, presented on a portable display. For ease of interpretation by the receiver, the pictographic symbols are accompanied by the written words they represent. Bliss symbols were originally developed as an international symbol system (Silverman, McNaughton, & Kates, 1978).

Picture boards are portable boards on which pictures or pictorial representations can be attached. Such communication boards have been in use for physically handicapped children for many years. Communication boards are limited by the number of pictures or pictographs that can be used at any one time, but they have useful functions in basic communication for children who have some sight.

The application of advanced and sophisticated technologies in the service of communication is creating a variety of new communication devices. New tools that utilize closed circuit television and electronic display boards are making it easier to select appropriate augmentative systems (see Chapter 8 for a more complete discussion of computer-aided communication systems).

In general, the faster and less cumbersome the system, the more desirable it is. Most children, especially older ones, prefer systems that are not large or obtrusive (Davies, 1984). Noncommunicating children begin to assert their own preferences once they have a means of expression.

Choosing a Symbol System

The choice of an appropriate symbol system may be problematic for children who combine visual and physical impairments. Symbol systems may be tactile, visual, auditory or a combination of two or more modalities, such as raised letter symbols. Symbol systems such as pictographs, pictorials, or whole words have the advantage of representing concepts. The more abstract (symbolic) the system, the more flexible it is. Some children may be limited to the concrete representations, while others are able to use abstract systems. As Beukelman, Yorkston, and Dowden (1985) suggest, nonspeaking individuals may need a variety of systems for different purposes. The communication needs and level of language comprehension of individual children determine the choice of system.

For example, 10-year-old Richard, who has oculomotor problems and is quadriplegic, was trained to use a communication board with large clear pictures. Richard's visual and physical problems made it difficult to assess his level of language comprehension. Careful observation indicated that he could make "yes" and "no" responses: He indicated "no" by pushing objects away, and "I want" by pointing to an item. Although Richard was not able to visually track moving objects, he was able to recognize large pictures of Coke, McDonald's hamburgers, French fries, and other familiar items. Large realistic pictures of food items were selected for training. Richard learned to respond to questions such as "What would you like to eat?" and "What did you eat for lunch?" by pointing to a particular food picture. He progressed from concrete food pictures to pictographic representations of activities. The choice of a symbol system for individual children depends on the following factors:

Communication needs of the student
The sense modalities the child actively employs
Level of comprehension of verbal language
Child's ability to read print or braille
Child's ability to make use of visual symbols, including those capable of being highlighted with color, contrast, or increased size
Child's ability to utilize touch as an input modality
Degree of hand control needed to read tactile symbols and ability of child to discern such symbols
Amount of training required for symbol interpretation
Versatility and flexibility of system

Summary

As Margaret Donaldson (1978) suggested, it is precisely because children can derive meaning from their environments that they are able to learn the symbolic codes that represent environmental events. Language learning and social interaction are intricately intertwined and interdependent. The aim of language intervention is to help children communicate meaningfully and spontaneously.

Speech and language development has roots in biological as well as social development. Language can only be acquired in a social context. Children learn to speak because they hear and comprehend language. The foundations of speech and language development are nonverbal communication and comprehension of the meaning of language forms. The ultimate goal of comprehensive language intervention is the communicative competence of individual children. Augmentative communication systems assist nonspeaking children to effectively communicate with their environments in order not only to respond, but also to initiate social contact and communicate wishes and desires. The chosen system must enable children to communicate in a variety of situations. The responsiveness of adults is a powerful tool in developing communicative competence.

Play and Social Interaction

Play is its own reward. Children play because they enjoy playing. The deep satisfactions and joyousness of children's play disguise its seriousness. Play gives children a way to confirm what they know about the world (Sutton-Smith, 1971). Play is so much a part of normal childhood experience that it is inseparable from other forms of spontaneous behavior. Play is exuberant activity; all aspects of life experiences are resources for play.

The absence of play behavior among children highlights its significance. Play is interaction; when there is no interaction, there is no play. The purpose of this chapter is to explore the value of play as a medium for developing self-awareness, social interaction, and social language. The topics to be addressed include the value of play in relation to cognitive and social development and a methodology for teaching children to play. The methods by which sensorimotor and social play are developed will be illustrated with anecdotal material.

The content of play is a rich resource for learning and interaction with the environment. Exploratory play is a medium for developing object knowledge; symbolic play is a medium for developing social interaction. Both of these forms of play are addressed.

Children who do not play express little spontaneity or joy in living; such children need to learn to play and become playful. These children seek control and maintain it by shutting out the outside world. Play is a medium of coaxing them into the world without taking control away from them. The answer to the question, "Can children be shown how to play?" is demonstrated by the children themselves. Play is learned behavior and is taught by nonjudgmental adults, who create the motivation to play and structure situations in which play can occur.

Play parallels children's efforts to expand their knowledge of themselves and the world they live in. Garvey (1977a) observed that play is most easily defined in terms of attitudes towards playful activities. The first and most important characteristic of play is that it is fun. Children play simply for the joy of playing. The goals of playing are in-

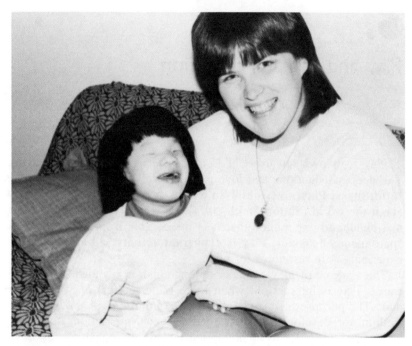

Amanda, a 5-year-old with anophthalmia, laughs with her teacher

trinsic and the motivation to play comes from the individual. Another characteristic of play is that it is spontaneous and voluntary. There is no obligation to play. Play expresses awareness and parallels the child's achievements in the sensorimotor, social, cognitive, and language domains (Garvey, 1977a).

Piaget (1962) considered three kinds of children's play. The first, sensorimotor play, consists of the varying actions and repetitions of the very young child seeking mastery of and control over objects and events. Fascination with cause and effect is characteristic of this level of play. Exploratory and manipulative skills are practiced as children play.

Symbolic, or make-believe, play is the next kind of play to develop. This is play with ideas and represents the people and events in children's lives. Symbolic play parallels the development of language and social skills. The third kind of play is represented by games, characterized by rules. Sensorimotor and symbolic play normally develop in the first six years of life. A review of the relationships of play to social and cognitive development is helpful in identifying the elements of play that make it so powerful a medium for encouraging and developing environmental interactions.

The Value of Play

The research on children's play illustrates the range of functional competencies enriched by play experiences. Play with objects teaches children how to explore and test their ideas about the world. Symbolic play builds a foundation for more evolved forms of symbolic activities (Piaget, 1962). Through play, children clarify and master fundamental skills and concepts (Isenberg & Jacobs, 1982). Sylva, Bruner, and Genova (1976), studying the effects of play on problem-solving skills, concluded that children who play freely, demonstrate problem-solving ability, goal-directed behavior, and persistence.

Children's play is a window on their motivational competence (Hrncir, 1985). The work of Yarrow and his colleagues (1979) demonstrated the relationship of motivation to intellectual competence. These researchers found that attentiveness, persistence, and social responsiveness were correlated with success in learning situations. Play, like language, encodes and represents all aspects of experience (Garvey, 1977a). The imagery of play reflects children's knowledge of familiar experiences. Pretending is a form of cognitive behavior; children's abilities to perceive the connectedness of events are revealed in their construction of play situations. Events must be perceived as connected before they can be reconstructed in play (Garvey, 1977a).

The relationships between objects and events are re-created in play. The progression from discovery and simple manipulation to the imaginative use of objects demonstrates a growing knowledge of connections and relationships. Simple play with a single object evolves into a sequence of play actions involving two or more objects. A child representing a sequence of play actions such as pretending to pour milk from a bottle into a glass and drink it, is relating one action to another action and one object to another.

Sutton-Smith (1971) suggested that there are four modes by which children come to know the world: imitation, exploration, testing, and construction. Each is represented in the development of children's play.

Imitation

The earliest forms of imitative play can be seen in the infant who attempts to imitate the facial expressions and actions of the mother. The child borrows from adult routines and imitates the actions of adults (Herron & Sutton-Smith, 1971). The first forms of "pretend" play consist of actions the child sees adults performing, such as talking into telephones, driving a car, eating, washing one's face, or going to sleep. The social routines discussed in the previous chapter are examples of imitative play. Imitation is an important learning strategy in the early years (Piaget, 1962). Through imitation children rehearse social behavior.

Exploration

Exploration is a powerful medium of learning; through the medium of playing, there is thorough investigation of the properties of objects. Containers are filled with water; paper is pulled, twisted, and torn; toys are tasted, banged, smelled, and fingered. Sutton-Smith (1971) noted that exploration only becomes play when children begin to use toys or other objects on their own. Exploratory play is a strategy of confirming ideas about objects and what one can do with them.

Testing

Children predict the outcomes of their actions by testing themselves or objects (Sutton-Smith, 1971). Climbing into cupboards or boxes and crawling over, under, and around things, are ways of validating experiences and testing. Children seek to understand the world by testing to see if their behavior will have predictable effects. As Sutton-Smith suggests, while exploration focuses on the objective world, testing emphasizes the subjective world and its possibilities (Sutton-Smith, 1971).

Construction of Experience

By the third and fourth year, children are able to build a make-believe world, complete with imaginary characters and events, and fashion their ideas from the fabric of their experiences. They come to understand the world by putting things together in their own ways. Pretending extends the child's domain of experience (Sutton-Smith, 1971). Imagination is nurtured by pretending. Toy props help to make the transition between real life and make-believe. As agent-action relationships are realized, they are represented in pretend play as well as in language (Hill & McCune-Nicolich, 1981). Bates and her co-workers (1977) reported that representational make-believe play emerges at about the same time as language.

Awareness that individual actions are part of larger, coherent activities is demonstrated as children combine their actions into packages of purposive activities (Garvey, 1977a). The first activities to be "pretended" are actions that are familiar and understood, such as eating, drinking, or sleeping. Rubin (1980) noted that children's understanding of a sequence of separate events can be observed in such dramatic endeavors as pretending a doll is sick. The sequence involves calling the doctor, putting the child to bed, getting medicine from the drugstore, and so on. These examples provide evidence of the cognitive underpinnings of dramatic (make-believe) play. Two kinds of social constructs are developed in dramatic play, first, the theme or story line, and second, the role to be assumed.

Play and Self-realization

Eyde and Menolascino (1981) identified several ways in which play facilitates personality growth. Through play, children imitate adults, rehearse real-life roles, and reflect feelings, relationships, and experiences. Of prime importance is the development of the "I am" and "I can" attributes of personality. "I am" aspects refer to the sense of self in relation to the environment. The "I can" aspects refer to the feeling of competence and control. Eyde and Menolascino (1981) state that self-understanding, self-mastery, and a sense of self-esteem are needed to confirm the "I am" and "I can" aspects of personality. As stated previously, these qualities are acquired through interactions with significant adults.

The realization of self as an autonomous independent person is marked by self-recognition in a mirror, the use of pronouns, and the ability to say "no" (Kagan, 1981). Children typically begin to recognize their own individualities and to assert their preferences in deliberate ways at about the age of 2 years. Recognition of the self in a world of other people presupposes the ability to think in symbolic or representational ways. Emde (1978) suggested that the use of the word "no" marks the shift toward thinking about oneself as an individual with one's own view of things. Make-believe (fantasy play) starts the process of stepping beyond one's own perspective and seeing events from another person's point of view. Rubin (1980) considers make-believe play to be an elementary form of decentration—the ability to step outside of oneself. Fantasy play, when it involves recognizable characters and story lines, becomes thematic or dramatic play.

Play nourishes the sense of self, while it allows exploration of the social roles of other people. Children explore relationships with other people in role play. The way they characterize the role reveals their perceptions of adults. Authority figures are portrayed as sympathetic, helpful, or bossy according to the way they are perceived. The discoveries children make about themselves and their relationships with other people are among the many social values of play. Garvey (1977a) noted that the principal resource for make-believe play is the real world as children know it. Socially learned expectations of the way people behave toward one another and the events of everyday living are the stuff of make-believe. When children play "house" or "hospital" or whatever, play allows them to explore the personal meanings of these events.

From Exploration to Make-Believe: The Sequence of Play Development

During the sensorimotor period of development, the environment can encourage or discourage the emergence of play behaviors. The mother who puts a toy boat in her child's bath and pushes it around in the water is creating a play event and showing her child how to play. Children learn to fit their actions to objects (Garvey, 1977a). They learn that balls can be rolled, pushed, kicked, and held; cups and glasses are for drinking, spoons and plates are for eating. As children become familiar with the uses of objects, they combine them into functional relationships. Spoons and plates are linked to the act of eating, soap and washcloths are linked to washing or bathing.

The notion that some objects are tools is acquired as children learn to use objects as tools or instruments. An increasing number of action patterns are combined to form larger coherent activities, such as cooking, dressing, getting ready for bed, taking a bath. Fantasy play, which is characteristic of children between the ages of 2 and 6 years, begins with simple pretending of single actions and progresses to more complex sequences, finally culminating in thematic play. As noted above, the first forms of make-believe are imitations of familiar actions. By the end of their first year, babies are imitating the actions of adults. Waving "bye bye," smiling in response to adult smiles, and many other facial expressions are examples of infants' imitations.

Fantasy play is true symbolic behavior, involving mental planning and the imagining of objects and events. McConkey (1984) identified a sequence of five stages in the movement from exploratory to fantasy play:

1. *Exploratory play*: The child plays with single objects.
2. *Relational play*: Two or more objects are combined in play.

3. *Self-pretend*: The child pretends an action such as drinking from a glass.
4. *Simple pretend*: The pretend actions are centered on objects, such as pretending to feed the doll.
5. *Sequence pretend*: The child pretends a sequence of actions, such as putting the "baby" (doll) to bed—placing it on a bed, putting a pillow under its head, and covering it with a blanket.

From about the age of 3 years, children engage in pretend play of a more structured character with two or more players. Role play combined with a play theme emerges. The themes of play are familiar events, such as family activities, cooking, eating, or going on a picnic. The theme is the focus of play and the springboard of activity (Garvey, 1977a). Each participant has a "play role." For example, when "playing house," each child takes a different role, such as mother, father, or child. Turn-taking and the structure of the play themes are shared among the participants. Fantasy play is truly social; even when a child is playing alone, a social role is portrayed (Garvey, 1977a). Children know when they are making-believe and have no difficulty distinguishing between play and reality.

The next stage in the evolution of play is the development of games. Games are governed by rigorous rules that involve team or group activities (Garvey, 1977a). Game play emerges after the age of 6 years, when children understand about cooperating and competing with other people.

Teaching Children to Play

All the reasons described above combine to make play an ideal medium for the development of interaction. Play has the power to motivate actions and demonstrate control over environmental events. Fun is its motivation. Making-believe offers rich opportunities for the dialogue relations necessary for true language communication.

Research on play among blind children suggests the strong role environment plays in encouraging play. Fraiberg (1977), Wills (1968), and others found gross delay in object play among blind children. The play of blind children has been described as less imaginative, less flexible, and more concrete (Warren, 1984). Rogers and Pulchaski (1984) studied the symbolic play of young visually impaired children and found that the children of playful mothers were more advanced in symbolic play than children who did not experience "playfulness." Rogers and

Pulchaski encouraged mothers to play with their children and found that symbolic schemata could be stimulated; their research suggested, however, that the beginnings of symbolic play may not be as easy for visually impaired children. Tait (1972) also suggested that blind children can be stimulated to play at age-appropriate levels. A study of play behaviors of visually impaired multihandicapped children demonstrated that such behaviors can be developed even by children with severe multiple handicaps (Rogow, 1981b). The verbal children in the study began to engage in active reciprocal play dialogue when teachers engaged them in dramatic or fantasy play.

The following discussion illustrates the process of children learning how to play. Small and tentative efforts combined to make a larger impact until finally there was true play complete with spontaneity and full participation. The play teachers were student teachers enrolled in a graduate program for specialist teachers of visually impaired children. The process of learning to play reveals the hesitations, the not-knowing or not-understanding, and the fear that insulates these children from interaction.

Although the activities defined as "play" have no extrinsic goals, the teachers had three well-defined goals for their students: stimulating interaction; developing play skills, including such verbal skills as dialogue and conversation; and encouraging spontaneous participation and child-initiated play.

The children described are severely visually impaired or congenitally blind and are all developmentally delayed. Some have physical and mental handicaps in addition to severe visual problems. The play sessions described took place weekly and the teachers kept detailed records of each play session. In addition, play progress charts were kept for each child. To record changes in participation in play, four categories of participation were used:

1. *Passive participation:* The child is spectator, indicating interest only by attending, holding a toy, or making a comment.
2. *Active participation:* The child imitates the actions of play, with motor action alone, with the use of a toy, or with verbal imitation.
3. *Active participation in thematic play:* The child participates by playing a role, such as "teacher" or "doctor," and contributes to the theme of play with activities, verbal expression, or active role play.
4. *Initiation of play:* The child creates a play theme and initiates play, showing spontaneity. The ideas come from the child.

Exploratory Play

Goal: To Develop Strategies of Exploring and Manipulating Toys.   Tracy, a 6-year-old, lived in a large institution. She was totally blind and physically very small for her age. Damage to her trigeminal nerve was believed to underlie the failure of speech to develop. Tracy had other physical problems as well, but her extreme aloneness and disinterest in the world were her most poignant and compelling characteristics. A play program was arranged in cooperation with the staff on the ward of the institution where Tracy lived. Tracy's teacher found the little girl sitting by herself in the corner of a large room, her head bent and her hands tucked in close to her body. She was motionless and seemed unaware of other children. When a toy was offered, Tracy refused to hold it and pushed it away. Her teacher noted: "Tracy needed so much. She needed to want to move around and explore her environment, to learn that it was interesting and fun to interact with other people. I decided to stress these goals" (Elgie, 1979).

The way Tracy was encouraged to play with toys demonstrated the importance of the adult in developing children's interest in and control of play events. Tracy first had to be shown how to play. Her teacher guided her hands over a series of toys and showed her how to turn, move, and twist them to make them work. To create motivation for holding toys, the play teacher held Tracy on her lap, speaking softly to her as she introduced a variety of musical toys. When Tracy showed interest in a musical clown that played a lullaby when its nose was twisted, her teacher decided to concentrate on that toy first. By showing interest, Tracy had made a choice. Her teacher took Tracy's hand in her own, and together they turned the clown's nose. Tracy listened to the music with her hand on the clown. When the music stopped, Tracy put her hand on the clown's nose. The teacher noted the gesture and turned the clown's nose again. As Tracy became familiar with the musical clown, her teacher placed *it in a bag* so that Tracy could find it by herself. When Tracy pulled it out, the teacher helped Tracy put the clown on her lap while she listened to its music. Tracy's permitting the clown to remain on her lap was interpreted as interest. This simple action served to give her control over the interaction with her teacher.

Tracy's enjoyment of music provided the clue to further motivation. Toys were chosen that either made music themselves or could be used to produce musical sounds. Toys that were not musical were introduced with a song or a rhyme. For example, Tracy was given a soft fluffy lamb while her teacher sang "Mary had a little lamb." Tracy held the lamb in her own hands. At each successive session, Tracy was given more time to explore each toy on her own.

Situations were created to shape anticipation. Song games such as "Hokey Pokey" were combined with a series of actions with the toys. As soon as Tracy heard her teacher's voice, she lifted her head and raised her arms, anticipating the play sessions. Tracy also began to use gestures as signals for particular songs or games. For example, she wiggled her toes to indicate that she wanted to play "This Little Piggy" or clapped her hands for "This Old Man."

Bells, keys, and other toys that made jingling sounds were tied on a string, so that Tracy could explore them independently. Her musical clown was given to her upside down and Tracy was shown how to turn it around. Hand-over-hand techniques were used to show Tracy how to turn the key or knob that turned the musical toys on or off. Interest and control go hand in hand. For example, Tracy's teacher turned on the musical clown and left it within her reach. At every session, she placed it farther away from where Tracy was sitting. Tracy never missed finding the clown and turning it on herself. Her teacher noted, "Tracy recognized my voice and my footsteps. She was always ready for play when I arrived. She communicated her preferences for songs and toys, and was active in initiating play" (Elgie, 1979).

The teacher brought a toy organ and showed it to Tracy. She played a song and then informed Tracy she was putting the organ in the toy bag. Tracy felt the bag, pulled out the organ, placed it on her lap, turned it about until it was right side up and the keys faced her, took her teacher's hands, and placed them on the keyboard. This was only one example of the many ways Tracy was actively participating, choosing, and enjoying play.

Goal: To Develop Concepts of Objects. The ability to form meaningful concepts of objects depends on experience with and mastery of objects. The way objects feel to the fingers, the sounds they make, the way they smell, their weight and temperature combine to form associations and meaningful concepts. Materials that require motor responses, such as toys on wheels and balls, lend themselves to concept building. A ball that can be held in the hand and that makes a sound as it rolls informs the child that an action has been performed on the toy. Knowing that a toy makes a sound when it rolls helps to locate the toy.

Randy was cortically blind and severely physically impaired. He had limited use of his left hand and arm. The 7-year-old boy had been abused by a mentally ill uncle when he was little more than a year old. His parents blamed themselves for having left him alone with the uncle and only wanted to make their son's life as comfortable as possible. Randy actively resisted any intrusion from the outside world. He had a set of wooden cars that he held in his left hand and jiggled. This was his only motor action.

Jiggling objects provides feedback only from the muscles involved in the jiggling action and supplies little information about the object itself. To Randy, the wooden car was not a car, but simply an object that could be jiggled.

The goals for Randy were to develop ideas about objects and what he could do with them. Teaching Randy to play illustrates the steps involved in helping a resistive and easily startled child to develop concepts of objects and associated actions. Toys were selected that would provide an immediate feedback, a sound combined with an action that would let Randy know he could cause an event to happen. Hand-over-hand techniques were used to show him how to handle toys.

His teacher spoke softly before touching Randy so that he would anticipate her approach. Since Randy liked to sit on the floor, toys were selected that could be moved along the floor. Rubber balls and smooth wooden toys with wheels were chosen. These toys were pleasant to touch and could be easily pushed or pulled. These toys could be heard as well as felt, combining listening with movement. Randy learned that if a toy had wheels, he could push it along the floor; if it had a string, it could be pulled.

Order and sequence contributed to concept development. Establishing an order for exploratory activities helps to build a reference point for action. Randy's teacher arranged a sequence of actions with particular toys so that the sequence itself could be used to develop mastery. Care was taken to see that Randy was able to relate sequence to outcome by stressing feedback and letting Randy experience cause and effect. His teacher wanted to make sure that Randy was developing a concept of related actions, rather than simply learning a rote sequence. As Randy acquired new skills, he became more willing to accept other toys. He was also encouraged to find new ways of using toys.

Balls did not always have to be rolled, they could be kicked or pushed. Before long, Randy began combining objects; he pushed a ball with a stick and used a toy car to roll it. He became interested in finding out how far he could push the ball. As he became more skillful, he increased the number of actions he could perform and experimented by pushing with his hand, his arm, or a stick. Using two objects together was an important discovery. His interests were expanding and it had become easy to introduce him to new toys.

As Randy gained awareness and skill, the teacher changed her role and became his play "partner," rather than a "manipulator" of the environment. As his teacher noted, "I had to be careful to lead Randy as far as he was able to go, and a little bit further, without either seeming to abandon him or stifling his new-found abilities." The toys that Randy had mastered were kept in a box, a visible indication of Randy's increasing mastery. He found the toys he wanted by himself and began to play even when the teacher was not present.

The behavior children exhibit after the play sessions often reveals what was learned. Randy began using his newly developed exploratory skills outside of the play sessions and became more attentive to other activities in school, as well as more accepting of change and transition (Balzarini, 1979).

Make-Believe Play

Goal: To Develop Concept of Role Play.   There are different types of role play. One type is a role defined by an action theme; if there is a car, for example, there must be a driver. The second type is defined by occupation or role. Playing "doctor," "teacher," or "mommy" involves character roles. The third type of role play is speaking for a puppet (Garvey, 1977a). Children know that when they assume a role in play, they are still themselves; they know that they revert to being themselves when the play is over. However, some children do not know how to play a "role" and must be taught, as was the case with 9-year-old Anna. The strategies used in teaching Anna to play illustrate how the adult can model role play for the child.

Anna is the only child of a single mother. She has some useful near vision but cannot see clearly beyond a range of three or four feet. When first encountered as a 9-year-old, Anna seemed like a much younger child. Fearful, resistant, and negative, Anna was a "loner" with little self-confidence. Her world was limited both by her handicap and her limited experience; Anna and her mother had little social life outside of the home.

Anna: I am the teacher.
Teacher: All right. You are the teacher.
Anna: You read your book now.
Teacher: I really don't want to read now. I want to talk to you.
Anna: You can't talk now. Don't you know that I am the teacher? This is my show.

Play with another person involves turn-taking and sharing ideas. At the beginning of the play program, Anna told her teacher that she did not like to play, trying to hide the fact that she did not know how to play. Familiar activities such as having a party, going swimming, riding a bus, or going to a market were used as play themes. Her teacher was careful to use activities that Anna knew and enjoyed in order to build her confidence. When the play sessions began, Anna was content to only physically manipulate the toys. Familiar roles and themes were modeled for Anna. The toy props were Barbie dolls, doll furniture, toy dishes, a toy stove and sink, and other familiar items.

Anna picked up the Barbie doll and held it close, feeling its hair and clothing. When her teacher suggested that they have a pretend party for Barbie, Anna agreed and even pretended to make the tea and then pretended to drink it. Anna was content to hold and touch the doll. She placed it on a shelf and then on the floor, saying, "Barbie is standing up. Barbie is sitting down. Barbie is on her bed." These brief descriptive statements were not followed by any further actions or play sequences. Her actions were unplanned and followed no sequence.

Dramatic play was modeled for Anna by giving roles to the Barbie dolls. Inflated plastic furniture was placed on one side of a table to represent Anna's "house." The teacher's "house" was set up on the other side of the table. Anna and her teacher agreed that they would be the "mothers" of the dolls. The following dialogue reveals how Anna began to get the feel of playing a role.

Teacher: (dialing a toy telephone) R-r-r-ing. This is Mary [the teacher's play name] speaking. Would you like to go swimming?
Anna: I want to come swimming.
Teacher: Can I speak to Barbie [the name of Anna's doll]?
Anna: Okay. Now I'm Barbie. I'm going swimming. Are you?

Anna found make-believe play fun as long as the activities were ones she enjoyed. Allowing the teacher to enter her play fantasy added some unpredictability to the situation, which Anna found threatening. She needed to feel that she was in control.

Anna set the table with toy cups and saucers and "made tea." She invited the teacher to her party and offered her a cup of tea.

Anna: Say you want sugar in your tea.
Teacher: No, I don't want sugar. I like milk in my tea.
Anna: No, you have to have sugar in your tea, just like me.

Teacher: Oh, when people play together, each person decides for herself.

Anna: All right, you can have milk.

Goal: To Develop Imagination.   The teacher maintained a "playful" stance and played in her "house," often inviting Anna to join her. When Anna began to accept using cardboard boxes and wire baskets instead of realistic play props, she was moved into a genuine play mode. Although she did not create play themes, the roles she played began to reflect more thought and imagination. A small cardboard box with a lid became Barbie's car and a wire basket was a swimming pool. Anna imitated her teacher in speaking for her doll and then initiated play roles for her doll. Soon she progressed to playing two roles simultaneously, changing her voice intonations. The daughter (Barbie) had a high-pitched voice, while her mother had a gruff voice and spoke in a domineering manner. Anna also "acted" for the two dolls. Anna had progressed from physical manipulation of the doll to creating a personality for Barbie.

Anna: (speaking into the telephone in her high-pitched "Barbie" voice) We are coming over to your house.

Teacher: All right.

Anna: We are going to play your piano. (Anna set her Barbie on the piano bench, and the doll slipped off.) Just a minute. We have to put Barbie to bed. We have to fix her foot.

Teacher: Should we call the doctor?

Anna: (in her gruff "Barbie's mother" voice) No. She'll feel all right soon after I give her a cookie. (Anna turns to the doll.) Now, don't be a baby. You shouldn't cry so much. You are really all right.

The play themes Anna suggested began to reflect some of her deepest concerns. Anna told her Barbie doll, "It doesn't matter if you feel afraid, the important thing is that you try to walk to school by yourself" (Kreiser, 1979).

Goal: To Develop Dialogue in Play.   Marie, a quiet, thoughtful 13-year-old, is blind in one eye and has peripheral vision in the other. Marie's family had immigrated from Portugal and she had only been in the school for two years. Marie's English was poor and she was placed in a special program for mentally handicapped children. Marie spoke in sentence fragments and would only respond to a request if it were preceded by her name. She did not initiate conversation. Because of her limited language skills, she was finding the school program difficult and frustrating. She withdrew into a sullen and stubborn silence when tense or agitated. At the beginning of the project, Marie was given three dolls in stylish teenage clothing. Play props—items of doll furniture such as miniature chairs and tables, beds, a telephone, and a toy kitchen—were arranged on the table that served as a play stage.

Marie gave each of her three dolls a name, sat them on the table in front of her, and spoke to each doll in turn. At first her conversation was descriptive.

Marie: Chris, you pretty. You blonde, long pretty hair. Frances, you pretty too. Pretty dress, pretty hair. Lily, you pretty, blue dress, feels nice.

Marie's teacher encouraged her to talk by pretending to be the dolls. She encouraged play action by creating play themes. For example, the teacher told Marie that they could all go to a restaurant; she gave Marie some plates and asked her to serve the dolls.

Marie: Listen to me. I am talking to you. Eat it. The food on the plate. Drink the cup through the mouth. Are you having a nice time? (After each question or comment, Marie waited as if the doll were replying) Yeah! By listening you can talk. (Turning to her teacher) My friends listen to me and they talk to me.

Her voice was animated when she conversed with her dolls. She laughed and smiled and enjoyed being the "teacher." Progress was recorded as Marie became more adventurous and began to create her own themes.

Marie: (talking to her dolls) I'm the teacher. Go play a game. What kind of game? (Waits for doll to finish talking.) Bingo.
Teacher: (talking for the doll) I won. Do I get a prize?
Marie: You won the big apple. (Turns to doll.) Now hold it in your hand. Yeah. That's good. Now eat it like this. (Demonstrates eating an apple for the doll.)
Teacher: (speaking for a doll) Can I watch TV?
Marie: Yeah. Look at TV. See, they are walking on ice with sticks and skates [ice hockey].

From simply describing events, Marie began to project ideas and feelings. She had given each doll a distinct personality. One of the dolls hated to go to school. Marie told her, "You have to be in school. You will learn to read and then you can to to the bank. Don't worry. One day you can be grown up and then you won't go to school."

Marie increased the quality and quantity of dialogue as she began to project her own feelings and ideas. Her play became a way of exploring emotions and human relationships (Cogburn, 1979).

Goal: To Explore Novel Situations.   Some children struggle to adapt to a sighted world and meet expectations that they act "normal" without ever understanding what "normal" means. Play permits a testing of self without having to know real fear.

Ricky was a tall and lanky 12-year-old whose mother worried about him constantly. His vision was extremely poor, although he had enough near vision to read print. His mother, thinking she was helping him, arranged Ricky's life in a way that allowed the smallest number of risks or uncertainties. Ricky's visual and physical problems kept him physically dependent on his mother's care. Ricky, like other children who lack spontaneity, often became upset in situations that were unexpected or unusual. He relied on other people to interpret the world for him.

Ricky was given a puppet who reminded him of Robin Hood, a favorite story. He was amused by the puppet, but showed no desire or ability to represent more than physical actions. His teacher suggested that they invite another child to participate in the play sessions. Ricky agreed. Tommy, a classmate of Ricky's, enjoyed puppets and was a good play model.

> *Tommy:* Robin Hood, can I go to the fair? Can I wear a suit of scarlet?
> *Ricky:* Your attention please. All archers report to the north side of the building.
> *Tommy:* I'm hungry. I think I'll go downstairs and get something to eat.
> *Ricky:* How come we have to fight when there is all this good food?
> *Tommy:* It belongs to the sheriff.
> *Ricky:* You used to come to do harm. This time you haven't come to do harm. You want all your silver back? Go home and wash it.

Ricky's new self-confidence was expressed by the personality and adventures of his puppet.

Other Considerations in Make-Believe Play.   As children gain play skills, they become more effective in playing roles, shifting from pure description to vivid interpretations of their roles. Lions become brave and ferocious, clowns become tricksters. The role of the teacher-model can be gradually faded as the children take more active roles. Modeling play for children may be more subtle than it first appears. If adult-models are too active, participation is discouraged and the child is placed in the role of audience. If they are not active enough, they fail to define and elicit active participation.

It is important to note that while language ability facilitates dialogue in play, limitations of language ability do not prevent play. Irene was 8 years old; she had only partial vision and was considered to be moderately mentally handicapped. Irene was initially passive, but quickly entered into active dialogue with her play teacher. Her limited language did not stifle her humor or her ability to vividly represent play roles.

Irene and her teacher were pretending to go to a picnic. The sweater and coat were make-believe.

Teacher: Are you dressed warmly?
Irene: No, cold.
Teacher: Here is a sweater. Are you warm now?
Irene: No. Coat.
Teacher: All right. You put on your coat.
Irene: Oh, heavy.
Teacher: Is it too heavy?
Irene: Too heavy.

Play themes that arise from familiar situations create opportunities for social interaction and direct language into social channels. Through dramatic play, children begin to take more initiatives, relate to adults, learn how to influence social situations, and turn their attention outward.

The Magic of Puppets

Puppets and dolls assist in the transition to role play. It is easier to give the role to a doll or puppet than to assume the role oneself. The puppet clarifies for the child the "pretend" nature of play and is therefore less threatening. The size of puppets and dolls allows children to feel more in control than they do when interacting with an adult. These qualities make puppets ideal for the teaching of role play. Children indicate their ability to project their feelings when they give life to their puppets, thus showing readiness for role play. Some children feel freer to let the puppet express their feelings than to do it themselves. Seven-year-old Frank wanted to be more physically active than his sight or physical handicaps would allow. Frank had a puppet named Sammy.

Frank: Did you know that Sammy is the bravest boy in the world? Sammy can jump off mountains and he can see all the way out to the sky. He can punch mean people. Sometimes I wish that I were as brave as Sammy.
Teacher: Oh, I think you're pretty brave, too.
Frank: Yeah, but Sammy can see. He can see as well as my Dad. He can walk pretty fast, too.
Teacher: You don't need to do those things to be brave.
Frank: I know, but when a person can see and walk real fast, they don't have to feel scared.

The essence of play—feeling free to express oneself—is something that many children experience most readily in musical activities that facilitate personal expression. In addition, song and rhyme are especially helpful in directing children's attention to words and meanings in playful ways. Music therapy, discussed in Chapter 4, can enhance and contribute to the development of play behavior. Not only do music and rhythm help children to organize their motor actions, but they provide motivation for playful activities. Rhythms combined with verse provide a structure for playful interaction. The structure of activity sequences develops anticipation and shows children how to participate. For example, poems or stories that talk about touching, feeling, reaching, and exploring can be recited while demonstrating the actions for the child. The adult recites the verse and uses hand-over-hand techniques to demonstrate the actions. The following story-songs (Dent-Cox, 1985) were created to encourage awareness of feeling and illustrate how touch experiences can be incorporated into play.

I SHAKE MY HANDS

I saw a feather fall from the sky.
It tickled my nose,
It tickled my toes,
It tickled me all over

Mimi enjoying puppet play

And when I am tickled I sing,
I shake my hands, I shake my hands,
I shake my hands all over.
I shake my hands, I shake my hands,
I shake my hands all over.

DIRTY DOG BLUES

The dog is too dirty
It's time for a bath.   (*wash child's body with soft cloth*)
And washa, washa, washa, like that.
First his head then his shoulders,   (*wash areas indicated*)
His arms and his knees
a washa washa washa that's clean.
The dog is not happy   (*sad voice*)
The dog starts to moan,   (*hand on hand, child slaps
no washa, no washa, no washa he groans.   knees or floor*)

The rhythms and poetry of these rhymes combine the modalities of
listening, feeling, and acting. They direct the child to listen to words
and combine them with appropriate actions.

Group Play

Discussion up to now has been concerned with adult/child play. In school, children spend much of their time in groups. Most of the play techniques that have been illustrated can be adapted to working with children in small groups. Peer play can be encouraged in much the same manner as play with adults. In some situations, as with Ricky, peers can be involved almost from the start. Play with puppets is uniquely adaptable to group play. The teacher working with small groups of children is able to develop and model play themes in much the same way as was done for individual children. As Sutton-Smith (1971) noted, children play because play is the most exciting activity there is. Other children are good play models and encourage participation without self-consciousness.

Encouraging Parents to Play with Their Children

Play is a medium of interaction for parent and child. Play is so easily adaptable to family routines that it can be made a part of the normal process of caring for the child. By playing with their children in a relaxed and comfortable manner, parents can achieve intimate and joyful moments with their children. Special times and places should be set aside for playing, and there should be a storage area for toys. The choice of time depends on the child and the needs of the family. Children should be in a position that will allow them to participate in play. Parent comfort and awareness of desired outcomes contribute to the success of play programs (Linder, 1982). The sequence from exploratory to make-believe play provides a simple means of guiding parents to the appropriate level of play.

Toys

Finding appropriate toys suitable for children with combined visual and physical handicaps is often a problem. Tactile, visual, and auditory attributes can be added to toys to make them more appealing. Physical modifications, such as increasing the size of the handles or attaching strings or bells, can make rather ordinary toys attractive. Miniatures and plastic imitations of objects, so appealing to the eye, have little meaning for visually impaired children.

An important criterion for the selection of toys is the sensory feedback they offer. Toys that combine sound with touch as well as vivid visual forms and color are likely to have a stronger appeal. Small cardboard or plastic boxes containing dried leaves and flowers, buttons, pieces of string, and paper to accompany simple stories about their contents make delightful toys. Fascinating storybooks can be created out of fabrics of different colors and textures. Sewing or pasting pockets onto the pages and placing little objects in them adds interest and an element of surprise to the books.

Jane Kronheim (1985) created toys she calls "learning pillows." Various items—small bells, materials of different textures, objects of different shapes, and little toys—are attached to square felt pillows. The child turns the pillow to discover more items. For example, one learning pillow tells the story of "Mr. Bug," who discovers jingle bells on the pillow and "Velcro that goes rip or zippers that go zip."

It is often necessary to spend time showing children how to manipulate and play with toys. When interest with play objects is established, cardboard boxes and other "make-believe" materials can be used. Toy props should stimulate imagination and interaction. Outdoor toys designed to stimulate gross motor development also encourage imagination.

Battery-operated toys have the potential of giving children with severe physical handicaps immediate and independent experiences with toys. These toys foster interactive skills by showing children that they can control the toys; they also promote the development of physical and manipulative skills needed for operating mechanical and computerized communication devices (Faulk, 1985). Imaginative battery-operated toys encourage exploratory behavior, visual tracking, and make-believe play.

Battery-operated toys move, light up, and produce sounds. Cars, trains, trucks, doll babies that crawl, and small animals are examples of toys that move. Toys that light up and produce musical or animal sounds can be movable or stationary. Most of these toys can be adapted for different types of switch mechanisms.

In addition to electronic toys, other techniques also encourage exploratory behavior. An example is the Velcro mitt or band that can be fitted to the hand or arm to encourage the grasping of toys (Faulk, 1985). Pieces of Velcro are attached to the mitt and to the toy. Toys that make sounds, have interesting textures, and provide meaningful sensory feedback are suitable for blind children.

Summary

Play is a powerful medium for developing social and environmental interaction. Teaching children to play requires playfulness on the part of the adult. Too much adult participation discourages the child from taking an active role, while too little robs the play of needed structure and the opportunity for adult play modeling. Play begins with environmental exploration and object manipulation. Symbolic play begins with simple pretending and develops into dramatic play complete with a play theme and role play. Dramatic play reflects the children's perceptions of social roles.

The cognitive and social values of children's play include knowledge of self and others, cause and effect relationships, and the relatedness of objects and events. Dramatic play enhances self-awareness as well as awareness of the roles of other people. Puppet play permits insecure and withdrawn children to assume play roles. For some children it is far less threatening to assign social roles to puppets than to assume them themselves.

Play with adults and other children has the added advantage of developing conversational skills and developing children's own interests. Toys that provide multisensory feedback and battery-operated toys that can be set in motion by the children themselves enrich the play of visually impaired children with physical handicaps.

7.

A Curriculum for Independence

Readiness for learning is shaped by the quality of social interaction. Interest in the workings of the world and mastery of skills are shaped by successful environmental interactions. The purpose of this chapter is to consider the functional skills necessary for environmental interaction, personal competence, and independence. Functional skills bring children to new levels of awareness and encourage interaction and feelings of personal competence. The chapter is concerned with vision enhancement, listening skills, orientation and mobility, and the use of adaptive equipment.

In order to function independently, children must understand their environments and be able to make predictions about environmental events. Making sense out of the environment is the first step in gaining independence. Meaning is relative in the sense that it changes from one context to another or from one developmental stage to another, but there is nothing relative about its function in life.

Vision Enhancement

Vision enhancement is a progression beginning with the development of awareness and attention. Corn (1983) developed a model of visual functioning that consists of three dimensions: visual abilities, individual characteristics, and environmental cues.

1. *Visual Abilities.* This dimension consists of five physiological components:
   Near and distance acuity
   Central and peripheral visual fields
   Oculomotor ability (i.e., mobility of the eye)
   Brain function—the occipital lobe and other areas of the brain that contribute to fixation, fusion, awareness of motion, and accommodation

Light and color reception; tolerance and perception of light intensity

2. *Individual Characteristics.* This dimension includes characteristics of the learner such as cognition, motivation, motor development, physical health, and stamina.

3. *Environmental Cues.* These are the visual attributes of objects, such as intensity of color, contrast, distance from the viewer, pattern, and inner detail.

Each of the three dimensions contributes to meeting the demands of visual tasks (Corn, 1983). Changes in one dimension alter the nature of the visual task. For example, increasing the size of the object may reduce the amount of time needed for its presentation. There are cognitive as well as sensory aspects to looking behaviors. From an educational perspective, the cognitive aspects are the goals of vision enhancement. Visual search, perception of form, visual interpretation, and hand/eye activities are expressions of the cognitive aspects of vision. They are what make visual experiences meaningful.

The sequence of visual development begins with oculomotor control, the ability of the eyes to fixate on still objects and track moving objects. Fixation and tracking involve the control of gaze and together form the first stage of visual development.

Visual Fixation and Tracking

At the earliest stages of visual development, the most important sphere of visual awareness is the near visual environment. Jose, Shane, and Smith (1980) suggest that visual tracking behavior be carefully observed to discover if the child is able to track, and, if so, how tracking is accomplished. For example, some children track to the midline and then stop. This is often the case when there is better vision in one eye than the other. Some children cannot use both eyes together.

Fixation is stabilized only when the eye muscles are brought under control. Children should be encouraged to use both eyes (if there is visual capacity in both). Guiding, urging children to look, and providing visual stimuli that they can see encourage fixation and tracking. A moving light, such as the light from a flashlight, is good stimulation for helping children to hold their eyes steady.

Fixation on objects coming into view indicates control of line of sight. It also indicates that the eyes can move in relation to an object. Objects used in vision enhancement should be turned in various positions and introduced both from the sides and from the front so that children become aware of different angles of perspective (Barraga, 1976).

Parents or teachers frequently observe visually guided behaviors among children diagnosed as "blind." In these cases it is imperative to find visual stimuli to which these children respond. A child may not respond to a penlight, but may react to a large white dot moving rhythmically on a television screen (Corn, 1983). Once the appropriate visual stimulus is identified, it can also be used to develop control of visual fixation and tracking. Vivid color contrasts, such as yellow and black, increased object size, and the elimination of clutter encourage visual responses.

Visual impairments have multiple effects on the ways individual children experience their vision. Two children with the same impairment, acuity, age, and experience may still experience their vision quite differently. Careful observation of the general conditions—type of environment, lighting, and angle of view—that prevail when individual children are making their best responses will provide helpful information. For example, some children require eccentric viewing techniques to enable them to see; they may need to bring the objects very close to their eyes, hold them off to one side, or tilt their heads.

Seven-year-old Teddy, who has Down's syndrome and congenital glaucoma, is a case in point. His vision fluctuates from hour to hour. The fluctuations are related to amount of available light, fatigue, and other factors. Teddy's best angle of view is his central vision, straight ahead. With his right eye, he can only see what is directly in front of him, on a straight line with his line of sight. His left eye gives him slightly more vision. Teddy can track a moving object with his left eye and distinguish between objects in the environment, but if something he has been watching disappears from his visual field, Teddy behaves as if it no longer exists. Teddy is more interested in what he sees than in what he hears or touches. His tactile skills are limited and his attention span is short. He relies more on vision than on other sense modalities. Therefore, the goals for Teddy were to develop efficient techniques of visual search and identification of objects in his immediate environment.

Teddy made good use of eccentric viewing techniques. He was shown how to keep his head straight and view objects by getting in front of them or holding them in front of his eyes. In this way, he was able to maximize his best field of view. Teddy began to search faces, smiling when people smiled at him and even imitating facial expressions. With improvement of visual skills came improvement in communication as well as tactile skills. By watching people when they spoke to him, he made his first efforts to imitate speech. Memory, recognition, and imagery developed as Teddy established visual contact with the environment.

Visual Recognition and Discrimination

There is steady progression from receiving visual stimuli to recognition, interpretation, memory, imagery, and association of visual stimuli with information from other sense modalities. Perception is enhanced by encouraging multisensory experience. Vision can be combined with touch and sound. Placing objects in positions close to the child or against contrasting backgrounds encourages visual search. As soon as the child shows recognition of objects, pictures and other visual displays can be used. Visual imagery and visual memory develop with increased and varied experience. Some children only begin to use their vision after visual impressions have become meaningful. The cognitive goals of vision enhancement and training include (Barraga, 1976):

1. Visual Discrimination:
   Form perception (discrimination among objects in the environment)
   Perception of details
   Purposeful scanning and strategies of visual search, such as looking at whole objects and relating parts to whole (visual closure)
2. Visual Imagery and Visual Memory
3. Complex psychomotor tasks, such as:
   Directing gaze in response to verbal instruction
   Hand/eye coordinated activities, such as cutting, drawing, and outlining

Listening Skills

Hearing, like vision, is a cognitive as well as physiological function. Listening skills are defined here as the use of hearing to interact with the environment. Listening to or listening for are important ways of finding out about the environment. The sounds of doors opening and closing, telephones ringing, footsteps, traffic, and airplanes remain empty sense impressions when no interpretations can be made. These sounds come from a distance. They cannot be reproduced until they

Visual perception training can be fun, too

reappear. The occurrence of these sounds is unconnected to children's actions and they are passive in relation to them.

Children become active listeners when they enjoy varied experiences with near sounds—sounds that occur close enough to them that their sources can be reached and touched so that the child can cause the sounds to be repeated. Active listening is encouraged when objects producing sounds can be touched. Awareness of objects in the near space is the first step in the use of objects. For very young or very passive children, placing many objects or toys around them increases their chances of finding objects and thus encouraging them to search.

Repetition, repetition, and more repetition create the necessary conditions for the beginning of experimentation with noises. As children develop associations between bodily movement, such as pressing a button, and the sounds they produce by that act, both movement and sounds become more meaningful. Developing awareness of sound and sound-producing events encourages spontaneous activity.

For the congenitally blind child, the sense of audition is the only one that brings information about the distant environment. Gayle's experience illustrates how sound recognition and sound localization can be encouraged in a severely handicapped blind child. This six-year-old is totally blind and has spastic cerebral palsy. She enjoys listening to music but is unaware of the sounds she herself can produce. Sound and touch were combined to develop awareness of environmental sounds. A plastic bowl filled with plastic balls was placed in front of her and hand over hand, her teacher showed her how to stir the balls in the bowl. This action provided a variety of sense impressions, combining hearing with movement and touch. By holding the bowl against her body, she could feel the vibrations as she moved the objects around. Different objects were placed in the bowl, reinforcing the association between object and sound.

When she began to hold the balls by herself and remove them from the bowl, she was ready for the next step. Gayle was encouraged to experiment with the balls, even throwing them on the floor to hear the sounds they made. The sounds of the plastic balls hitting the floor helped her to develop a sense of space and direction. Picking up and holding objects was carried into other situations, such as holding her own soap while washing, or her own eating utensils during meals.

Orientation and Mobility

Orientation and mobility skills make it possible for blind children and adults to function with safety, efficiency, grace, and independence in both indoor and outdoor environments (Hill & Ponder, 1976). Lowenfeld (cited in Hill & Ponder, 1976) defined mobility as a capacity or facility for movement that is made up of two components: the ability to recognize one's surroundings, and a means of locomotion from one place to another. Teaching independent mobility to visually handicapped children and young adults who are nonverbal and who may have additional developmental handicaps requires modification of techniques and methods of instruction. The techniques and methods described in the following section are based on the work of Berdell Wurzburger, who has demonstrated that even the most severely handicapped child can be shown how to move with confidence and safety.

Berdell Wurzburger's contributions to mobility instruction for multiply and developmentally handicapped blind children deserve special acknowledgement. He developed his methods in the corridors and on the grounds of the Sonoma Developmental Center (formerly Sonoma State Hospital) in California and Woodlands, a provincial institution for mentally retarded people in British Columbia. Under his guidance mentally handicapped blind persons who were barely able to walk when training began learned to walk with independence and confidence.

Orientation and mobility training teaches children to negotiate the physical environment. Successful implementation of such a program requires sense training and the development of body image and environmental awareness. The following definitions are helpful in understanding orientation and mobility instruction.

Orientation: The use of the remaining senses, including vision, to determine position in the environment.

Mobility: Knowing how to move safely from one known location in the environment to another known place.

Orientation and Mobility Training: Teaching children to coordinate all their sense impressions in order to know the environment and move safely within it; such training is provided by certificated instructors who have taken a prescribed course of Orientation and Mobility instruction.

Landmarks: Familiar objects, sounds, odors, and temperature or tactile clues that are easily recognized and constant. They must have known, permanent locations and serve to identify a particular place (Hill & Ponder, 1976). Landmarks may be anything—buildings, bushes, furniture, or sound-producing objects such as ticking clocks—that establishes a reference point for movement from one location to another.

Guidelines/Shorelines: The edges formed where two surfaces meet, such as a lawn and a sidewalk, the curb and the roadway, or the walls and the floor.

Trailing: Using the back of the hand, the fingers, or a cane to follow a shoreline and thus find landmarks, determine direction, or move in a parallel line. Typically trailing is accomplished by placing the back of the hand lightly along a wall.

Squaring Off: The act of aligning and positioning one's body in relation to an object for the purpose of getting a line of direction (usually perpendicular to the object) (Berdell Wurzburger, personal communication, 1987).

Protective techniques: Hand and arm postures used for protection against bumping into things such as partially opened doors (Hill & Ponder, 1976).

The Long Cane: A prescription cane used as an obstacle detector. It was developed at Valley Forge Army Hospital by Richard Hoover, and its length is determined by the height of the user and length of stride (Berdell Wurzburger, personal communication, 1987).

Echolocation: The use of reflected sound to orient oneself in space. Sound bounces off buildings and other environmental objects, and one can learn by listening to emitted or reflected sound. Some children stamp their feet or click their tongues to receive an echo feedback.

Sighted Guide and Trailing

Orientation and mobility instruction is sequenced. Students are first shown how to move with maximum protection. Sighted guide and trailing are the first two phases of traditional mobility instruction.

The *sighted guide technique* is the first step in mobility training— teaching students to follow the movements of a human guide. The student is positioned one half-step behind and to the side of the guide, with the student's shoulder in a direct line behind the shoulder of the guide. The student holds the guide's arm just above the elbow, allowing the guide's hands to be free for opening doors. Maintaining this position is especially important when turning corners and making turns so that the student does not move beyond the protection of the guide.

Learning to *trail* is the next important phase of traditional mobility training. Trailing is the act of using the fingers or back of the hand to follow a surface. As described by Hill and Ponder (1976), trailing allows the student to:

Determine position in space
Locate a specific object
Maintain a parallel line of travel

Trailing can be aided with the use of soft ropes to guide the student along a pathway.

Wurzburger (personal communication, 1987) advises that sighted guide techniques do not offer enough security for some students; if the student resists working with a sighted guide, it is wise to go directly to cane techniques. In specialized environments, cane mobility is probably the safest and preferred mode of travel.

Adapted Cane Techniques

Independent use of the cane is the third phase of traditional training. Functioning as an extension of the hand, the long cane, or "white cane," is used to probe the immediate terrain. With the cane, the user is able to detect drop-offs, obstacles, bumps, curbs, and steps. The arm receives the information through the correct position of the cane (Croce & Jacobson, 1986).

Learning to use the long cane for independent mobility

The majority of the skills acquired during mobility training involve complex motor skills, such as learning to grasp the cane, hold it waist-high at midline, and swing it in an arc. Several different motor skills must be attended to simultaneously. As a general rule, learning a new motor skill requires that the skill be practiced enough to become automatic (Croce & Jacobson, 1986). Even blind students who have little difficulty with academic tasks may find it difficult to learn cane technique.

In the beginning stages of cane-travel, the child is taught to position the cane diagonally across the body and to maintain this position while walking. After students have become adept at walking with the cane held diagonally in one hand, they are taught to switch hands. As proficiency is gained, students begin to learn the "touch" technique, which involves swinging the cane in an arc and lifting it slightly from the ground.

Wurzburger made several important adaptations to traditional cane techniques for his students. The goals for teaching developmentally delayed blind students are, in Wurzburger's words, to "Get them up, get them moving, and make the training as easy and concrete as possible!" In order to achieve these goals, Wurzburger (1) introduced the constant contact technique, (2) used weighted canes, and (3) switched immediately to the use of canes for those students, typically the most insecure nonverbal learners, who were unable to make good use of sighted guides.

The "constant contact" technique involves moving the cane in an arcing pattern without lifting it from the ground. Holding the cane to the ground permits increased and continuous feedback from the cane. A large plastic tip, the "marshmallow" tip, is attached to the end of the cane to further intensify the feedback (Berdell Wurzburger, personal communication, 1987).

The canes are weighted by placing lead weights inside them. Weighting discourages students from lifting their canes. As students learn to maintain contact with the ground, the weights are gradually removed.

Other adaptations, such as the use of plastic rope or tape to mark indoor and outdoor pathways, serve to outline pathways and encourage independent and safe movement in previously unknown environments. The act of grasping the rope gives some students more confidence than trailing. Plastic tape that can be felt by the foot assists in the recognition of particular environments (Berdell Wurzburger, personal communication, 1987). These techniques make it possible for severely and multiply handicapped children to acquire mobility skills.

The extent to which mobility skills need to be broken down into their subcomponents depends on the students' performances (Croce & Jacobson, 1986). Hand-over-hand demonstrations are necessary for students with poor or no language skills. For children with good language skills, instruction can be verbal as well as demonstrative.

A review of the techniques used with Peter, who had never walked alone before receiving mobility instruction, illustrates how mobility goals can be translated into daily instruction. He was 15 years old when we first met him. His family came from Hong Kong. Peter had never been to school before coming to Canada. He is congenitally blind due to severe retinal disease associated with a rare chromosomal disorder. Peter has had several seizure episodes and is on daily medication; otherwise he is in good health. Peter's parents truly believed that he would never be able to do anything for himself, and so they, along with his brothers and sisters, catered to his every need. They simply wanted Peter to be comfortable and happy.

Before training began, Peter's favorite position was to curl up in a comfortable chair, with his legs crossed and pulled up to his chest and his arms wrapped around his body. In this position he had minimal contact and interaction with the environment. Although withdrawn and silent, Peter was able to follow such instructions as "stand up," "hold on," and "give me your hand," as well as some other phrases. He could hold objects in his hands, use eating utensils, push buttons, and button his shirt, but he tended to do everything with one hand. Bimanual coordination was not observed. There was evidence of weakness on one side of his body; he dragged his right leg when walking. With slouched posture, shoulders hunched, and head tilted, Peter shuffled rather than walked. The mobility goals set for Peter were the following (Yakura, 1986):

1. *Use of Sighted Guide.*   Peter learned to loop his hand through the guide's arm. Because his right side appeared weaker than the left, he was guided from the right to give him additional support.

2. *Trailing.*   Peter learned to trail using a rope railing, which was put in place in the corridor of the school. Trailing a wall proved more difficult, but with hand-over-hand techniques and practice, Peter learned to trail using both the rope and the wall. He responded well when his teacher walked behind him. When the teacher was in front he tended to hold on to her.

3. *Doors.*   Peter tended to stand at entranceways, such as doorways leading from classroom to hall or hallway to cafeteria, as if he did not realize that he could go through the door and continue his course of travel. He was given a great deal of practice going in and out of doorways holding his left arm across his chest (as a protective technique), until he learned to walk through doorways without hesitation.

4. *Cane Technique.*   Peter was shown how to use the cane in constant contact with the ground to give him maximum feedback. Arcing techniques were not introduced. Using the cane with his left hand, he discovered its value for himself and became proficient at finding steps and curb drop-offs. One day, his teacher observed him stamping on a wooden floor after he left a carpeted area. He was beginning to develop his own techniques of learning about the terrain. On daily walks, Peter improved both his knowledge of routes of travel and his cane skills. He learned to travel alone from the parking lot into the school building and back.

The experience of another student, Ronny, shows how good cane technique can be mastered by nonverbal mentally handicapped students. Ronny, a congenitally blind 19-year-old, has been a resident of an institution for the mentally handicapped since he was 8. Fearful of walking on his own, Ronny moved very slowly, clicking his tongue as he walked along outdoor paths. While he enjoyed being outdoors and made good use of echolocation, he rarely walked outdoors on his own.

A mobility program was formulated for Ronny that had two goals (Sparrow, 1986). The first was to get Ronny to maintain constant contact while arcing the cane. Ronny was taught cane technique using a weighted cane because he had a tendency to lift the cane from the ground. Hand-over-hand assistance was initially required, but was soon replaced with verbal reminders such as "over" and "back." After a few weeks of practice, Ronny discovered the freedom the cane gave him and began to pay attention to his handling of the cane. He learned to hold the extended cane beside his right hip and use the constant contact method.

The second goal of the program was to teach Ronny to use the cane to detect obstacles in the path. His teacher guided him towards obstacles such as benches, fire hydrants, or large wastepaper baskets. He was guided hand over hand to explore obstacles with his cane. After a few weeks of training, Ronny began to notice the obstacles on his own. For example, there was a bench in the path, and Ronny held out his cane to explore it. When the teacher praised him, Ronny grinned and patted the cane as if to say, "See what a great help this cane is" (Sparrow, 1986).

Mobility training contributes to great improvement in self-confidence, physical coordination, fitness, and endurance.

Adapted Mobility Skills for Less Ambulatory Students

For students who are in wheelchairs or use crutches or walkers, further adaptations are necessary. Seeley and Thomas (1966) taught mobility to a congenitally blind girl who walked with crutches. The 12-year-old girl had normal intelligence and attended a junior high school. Sighted guide and trailing techniques were adapted to her capabilities. Instead of holding on to a guide's arm, the student was taught to follow the sound of the guide's voice and footsteps. The guide gave her information about turns, directions, stops, and obstacles in the path. In order to trail, the girl was taught to take several steps on her crutches and then check with one crutch to make sure she was close to the wall. Routes were planned that allowed her to stay in contact with a wall or other landmark as much as possible. Trailing in this manner permitted her to locate doorways and openings along the walls. The student used both her crutches during mobility training so she would be able to maintain balance with either one while trailing with the other. At the end of the training period, she had learned to get around most of the school building on her own.

Similar adaptations can be made to teach mobility to children who use walkers or wheelchairs. The students should be familiar with the use of their equipment before training begins, knowing, for example, how to turn the wheels of the wheelchairs or manage the walkers. Recommended first steps for walker users include learning to:

Get up from chair using the walker
Transfer from one chair to another, using the walker to walk between chairs
Walk alongside walls so they can be felt with one hand
Keep the walker on path by following the voice of the guide
Trail while avoiding obstacles
Make turns
Open doors

Recommended first steps for wheelchair users include learning to:

Trail a clear path
Locate doorways
Detect obstacles
Avoid obstacles
Make turns
Open simple doors
Transfer from the wheelchair to another chair independently

Mobility with Deaf/Blind Children

Mobility with deaf-blind persons presents another set of unique problems. Hearing loss does not prevent a child from enjoying the benefits of mobility training. Wurzburger found that the immediate introduction of a weighted rigid cane fitted with a marshmallow tip is the most efficient way to begin. Hand-over-hand techniques combined with making the pathways as safe and concrete as possible is helpful. The first route chosen should be simple, with few turns or stairways. Extra markers can be placed along the path at frequent intervals to reassure the students as they go from marker to marker to complete their routes. Few skills contribute as much as mobility does to feelings of personal competence and independence.

Teaching Concepts Related to Mobility

Some blind students may not know what a city block is or how houses are situated along a street. This kind of understanding is basic to outdoor mobility. It is important to target specific concepts when considering what children need to learn (Hall, 1982). Learning can be made easier by determining what the student does understand and then building on that understanding.

Locating objects in the environment requires understanding positions of things in relation to oneself. For example, although Eddy had good language skills, he had little understanding of spatial relations. The meanings of spatial terms such as "in front of" or "behind" were beyond the scope of his experience. The goal for Eddy was to become aware of the position of objects in relation to his own position. Since Eddy could localize sound, his teacher used her own voice to teach spatial relations. She would stand in various places in the room and ask Eddy to tell her whether she was in "in front of" or "behind" him. His instructions were to keep his head straight and use the words "in front" or "behind" to indicate the direction of her voice.

Prosthetic Equipment

Prosthetic equipment enables children to gain greater control over their movements and encourages interaction. Children who have handicaps that curtail their physical control need tangible forms of assistance with physical interactions. Prosthetic equipment that can be tailored to the needs of individual children can be divided into two categories: (1) nonprescription equipment, such as stand-up tables, prone boards, and other devices that offer adaptability, and (2) prescription equipment, such as positioning chairs that must be individually designed and fitted.

Positioning chairs can be designed to give children the opportunity to sit erect and experience the world from a different perspective. Green (1986) suggested that backs of the wheelchairs be padded with 1-inch foam rubber and Naugahyde for maximum comfort. Chest and head supports and detachable neck pillows attached to these chairs enable children who do not have head control to hold their heads upright. Green also suggested that ventilated wedge seats be contoured for the child so that weight is evenly distributed along the thighs, thus relieving back pressure. Elevating the knees by ½ to 2 inches can prevent scissoring of the legs. For children who are extremely thin or have severe deformities, a cut-out seat may be used. This type of seat reduces pressure on the bony portion of the buttocks. Velcro straps attached to the chair can be used to stabilize leg tremors without interfering with movement of arms and hands in voluntary actions (Green, 1986).

Well-designed position chairs help children to interact with their environments. A position chair can be fitted with other devices to maintain head control and allow children to use their vision. Specially designed walkers enable movement within the environment even for children who have very limited control. When properly designed and tailored to the individual child, such adaptive equipment can liberate children from many of the strictures imposed by handicapping conditions. As Green (1986) emphasized, it is important to have different kinds of equipment for different kinds of activities. Equipment can be used to prevent or lessen deformities as well as to improve performance in daily activities (Green, 1986). Another category of supportive devices, electronic aids, will be discussed in the next chapter.

Summary

A curriculum for independence aims to develop competence and mastery over environmental interactions. Most children with visual handicaps have residual vision, which in many cases is ignored. Vision is so important a sense in gaining knowledge of the environment that concentrated efforts to help children make use of their residual vision are an important part of functional curricula. Orientation and mobility training is another essential component that enables safe and independent movement within the environment. Mobility training for visually impaired children with additional handicaps requires some modification in both training procedures and environment. Wurzburger's principle of getting children up and moving is a realistic goal for even the most severely and multiply impaired individual. When the environment is fitted with markers, such as plastic ropes and tape on the ground, and weighted canes and the constant contact method are employed, it does not take long for blind children and young adults to gain confidence in movement. Adapted equipment that allows severely physically handicapped individuals to control their posture and improve their mobility can help to maximize environmental interaction.

8.

The Promise of Technology

Electronic technology is the magic of the present day. Its promise is to provide both the tools for communication, interaction, and academic learning for severely handicapped children and the media through which nonspeaking children can communicate and interact with their environments. Electronic tools are bridging the gaps between the abilities of children and the demands of their environments. The list of equipment made available by technological developments already includes computers and reading devices that speak, amplification and magnification devices that provide immediate access to written materials, and communication and prosthetic devices that override handicap. The purpose of this chapter is to illustrate how electronic systems can be harnessed in the service of access, independence, and achievement, with a focus on two main areas of application: instruction and communication. Prosthetic devices, such as speech aids and technical living aids, are also described.

All the devices and systems described in this chapter are currently available and suitable for visually impaired children. However, the field of technology is rapidly changing, and equipment is constantly being improved and replaced. Given what has already been accomplished in this area, its future role in the service of handicapped people is likely to be an extremely important one.

Electronic aids must be selected for the use of individual students, and there is no intention in this chapter to recommend one device over another. In instances where more than one company produces a given type of device, the generic name of the device is used; when equipment is available from only one source, the name of the manufacturer is included. It is beyond the scope of the chapter to deal with the technical and design aspects of the devices described.

The new technology is already making a profound difference in children's lives. Eddy, who was introduced at the beginning of this book, was unable to work in braille due to physical limitations in the range of motion of his hands. With a microcomputer hooked up to a speech output device, Eddy is writing his own compositions and studying mathematics and social studies in a junior high school. Diana, who is unable to speak, is doing advanced mathematics with a micro-computer hooked up to a large print display. Leanne, who has both visual and hearing handicaps, is using a computer for college courses. Paul, who was paralyzed and left with partial sight and impaired speech after a severe head injury, is back at his own school with a computer to act as his pencil and workbook. Geoffrey, with partial vision and severe physical handicaps, was thought to be profoundly retarded un-til he was taught to communicate with the aid of a computer. These children demonstrate how computer technology is being harnessed in the service of communication and learning.

Computers as Instructional Aids

The most well-known and adaptable electronic system is the micro-computer. Microcomputers offer many different kinds of advantages to children with special needs. Their capacity to interface with other types of audiovisual equipment, such as videotape recorders, voice synthesizers, and character readers that read existing print, make them adaptable to a wide range of instructional and communication uses. Microcomputers are capable of minimizing and even counteracting the effects of disability (Budoff, Thormann, & Gras, 1984).

In addition, the computer aids instruction in more subtle ways. It is neither critic nor judge and has infinite patience with the slowest and unsteadiest of learners. The computer teaches patience and precision as it provides immediate feedback and reinforcement. It is a machine that even severely impaired children can learn to manipulate. No other piece of equipment can compare with the microcomputer in the vir-tually limitless possibilities it offers in the service of access, inde-pendence, and achievement (Budoff, Thormann, & Gras, 1984).

Computer-based technology has its own language. The following definitions are helpful in describing electronic technology.

Communications: The means by which information can be transmit-ted between one computer and another or between a computer and peripherals.
Peripherals: Input and output devices, disks, tape drives, and termi-nals.
Interface: A mechanism that allows communication between two units not specifically designed for each other.

Hardware: The physical machine and its parts. Almost all hardware operations are controlled by software.

Software: The general term for programs that tell the computer what to do. The *menu* offered by the software lists the functions or options made available by the particular program.

Keyboards: Typewriter-style arrays of alphabetic and numeric switches that are the most widely used input devices. Variations among keyboards include the size of key tops and the shape of keys. A membrane keyboard uses a flat surface with printed keys, rather than raised, separate keys.

System switches: Control devices designed to put data into the system without the use of a keyboard. Visually and physically handicapped children may need to interact with the computer by means of a variety of switches that bypass conventional keyboards. Joysticks, widely used in video games, can be adapted for use by physically handicapped users. The joystick can be tilted in any direction and can be used as a pointer to indicate selected answers or messages. Other types of switches can be manipulated with the head, hand, foot, or tongue; indeed, such mechanisms can be adapted to respond to almost any control movements a child can make.

Voice synthesizers: Devices that produce recognizable speech through a speaker and interface with computers and communication equipment. They have particular application to blind students.

Computer Components

There are three basic components of nearly all computerized systems: input, processing, and output (Beukelman, Yorkston, & Dowden, 1985). The input component, which determines how the user interacts with the system has two aspects. The first of these is the mechanical means by which the system can be operated. The standard keyboard is the most conventional type of control. Other methods of control are switches, buttons, or even voice-operated control mechanisms that allow the user to command the system. For children who cannot use their hands, switches are available that respond to the blink of an eye, movements of the head, controlled breathing ("sip and puff"), or even the flexing of a muscle.

The choice of which type of switch to use depends on the motoric and visual ability of the user. Children who have head and hand or foot control may employ multiple switches or a joystick. For children with minimal physical control, a single switch combined with a scanner is frequently recommended (Beukelman, Yorkston, & Dowden, 1985). For those with severe visual impairments, a Morse code system combined with a pillow switch may be preferable. These methods are the means by which the user actually controls the computerized system.

The other aspect of the input mechanism is the symbolic system that is used to represent the information to be entered. These symbols, which usually appear on the keyboard when that device is used for input, can range from standard English letters (the most common) to braille symbols, words, phrases, or pictorial symbols. In systems based on Morse code, the symbols are not displayed and must therefore be memorized by the user (Beukelman, Yorkston, & Dowden, 1985).

The second basic component of computerized systems, processing, refers to what the system actually does with the input—what functions it is able to perform (Beukelman, Yorkston, & Dowden, 1985). Sophisticated systems are capable of both storing and retrieving information; simpler systems can only perform single functions. For example, the electronic calculator can perform a variety of mathematical functions, but it does not store information for future use.

Output, the third component of computerized systems, can take a variety of forms. Some systems can produce only regular, typed print-outs, while others have the capability for large print. Still others can create "print-outs" in braille. In addition to such permanent records, output may also be transitory, as is the case with visual messages flashed on a CRT screen (Budoff, Thormann, & Gras, 1984). Another transitory output mechanism, synthesized speech, has particular value for blind children.

Computer-Assisted Instruction

Budoff, Thormann, and Gras (1984) use the term "scenario" to describe an educational plan that includes a computer as a central component. The scenario may involve the use of a computer to motivate the student, to reinforce what has already been learned, to introduce new material, or a combination of all three. Computer use requires careful planning; appropriate software must be selected and the role of the computer in the student's overall instructional plan must be clearly defined.

Using the microcomputer in the classroom requires teachers to have a basic understanding of the technology and the particular qualities of each medium (Budoff, Thormann, & Gras, 1984). Visual media must be selected with care for visually impaired students. White print on a black background facilitates reading for some children. Others need large print and a reduction of the number of words displayed on the screen. Still others require a combination of both. While visual media have the advantage of providing immediate feedback and a vivid display, many children have problems with visual scanning. Audio output is an available alternative, but audio scanning requires that the student be able to memorize the selections on the menu.

Software programs hold the key to the success of computer programs. If students with complex handicaps are to be able to operate the computer independently, consideration must be given to the following questions.

1. *Is the program adaptable to the skill level of the student?*   The need to match the skill level of students with the demands of the program requires teachers to have sufficient technical knowledge to select appropriate software and make the necessary adaptations.

2. *Does the program allow for adjustments in level of complexity and/or rate of presentation?*   Spelling, reading, and language programs that can be adjusted to the student's level of comprehension are the most adaptable.

3. *Is the display readable?*   While there have been great improvements in the software available, programs specifically designed for visually impaired students are not easily found. A good software program provides uncluttered displays, adjustable letter size, and strong contrast.

4. *Is the program "user proof"?*   Recommended programs should be designed so that inadvertent pushing of a single key does not destroy the work the student is doing.

5. *Is the program "user friendly"?*   The software should be easily managed and free of "bugs" so that it runs as intended.

6. *Does the program include a way of recording students' progress?*   A good program also maintains a record of students' progress.

7. *Does the program provide immediate reinforcement for correct and incorrect responses?*   Immediate reinforcement encourages persistence. Simple messages, such as "good job" or a musical tone in response to a correct answer or a razzing sound in response to an error, add an element of fun and anticipation to computer use.

8. *Does the program encourage independence?*   Some software programs are specifically designed to allow students to experiment and discover some of the capabilities of the computer for themselves. An example of a motivating way to begin computer training is "Hodge Podge" (produced by Dynacomp, Inc.), which encourages experimenting with the keyboard. As a key is pressed, a song is played or a still or animated picture is presented on the screen.

9. *Can the program be used by totally blind students?*   Several different types of synthetic speech terminals that may be connected to standard microcomputers are currently on the market. Noteworthy among them is the Talking Terminal, produced by the Kurzweil Company of Cambridge, MA, which converts computer-transmitted English text into easily comprehended synthetic speech. Microcomputers have also been adapted for braille input and output. The VersaBraille, a sophisticated microcomputer that can be attached to another computer or used by itself, has both input and output capabilities. The user brailles the data onto cassette tapes capable of recording up to 400 pages. The VersaBraille is manufactured by Telesensory Systems of Palo Alto, CA, and is suitable for those who can read and write braille.

10. *Is training required in order for the student to use the control mechanisms efficiently?*   Physically disabled children often need training in the use of switches in order to establish the motor patterns required for computer use. The process that enables a child to predict the consequences of motor activity so that the intended consequences are achieved is called motor thinking (Beukelman, Yorkston, & Dowden, 1985). For example, motor thinking is involved in knowing how to turn switches on and off or move them to the left or right. The physically disabled computer user must be able to predict the effects of moving the controlling devices. As Beukelman, Yorkston, and Dowden (1985) suggest, physical and occupational therapy, as well as recreational activities, should be used to establish the motor patterns necessary for computer and other system use.

Electronic Devices for Visually Handicapped Learners

Eddy, who is blind and has cerebral palsy, had no way of writing until he was introduced to a computer. Eddy needed a system that would enable him to interact directly with a computer so he could do his own writing. A microcomputer adapted for Morse code input and attached to a speech output device provided the necessary medium. Eddy was first taught Morse code so he would be able to command the computer; the dots and dashes of the code were translated into time units of pressure on a pillow switch. As soon as Eddy mastered the Morse code, he was shown how to use it to instruct the computer. The speech output device attached to his computer lets Eddy know what he has written. Eddy is now writing compositions and reports for English and social studies at a junior high school. The computer has become Eddy's pencil.

The extent of 12-year-old Geoffrey's motor disabilities disguised the quickness of his mind and the extent of his comprehension. Geoffrey's speech was laborious and slow. It wasn't until Geoffrey was enrolled in the special class at his junior high school that he had access to a computer. His teacher, a computer enthusiast, immediately recognized the value of computer training for Geoff. Despite his slowness on an electric typewriter, Geoff was good at spelling and could write simple sentences. A computer specialist from a nearby rehabilitation hospital was consulted. At first a conventional keyboard was used. Geoff's vision was good enough to enable him to read the monitor, which utilized a black background with large white letters. The size of the letters and the contrast enabled him to read and correct his own writing, which he had been unable to do with the typewriter, but his finger movements caused him to make many errors. With the help of an adapted keyboard and a head switch that allowed him to provide various instructions to the computer, Geoff made dramatic progress. Through the medium of his computer, the full extent of Geoff's real abilities became apparent.

These are but two examples of the impact that the new technology is having on the lives of visually impaired people. In order to bring together people with disabilities and technology appropriate to their needs, it is necessary to know what is available and how it functions. The discussions that follow outline the major trends in the development of devices to assist visually and multiply impaired individuals.

Reading Devices

The inaccessibility of conventional reading material has long plagued the education of visually impaired children, but new reading devices are beginning to overcome the barriers imposed by print materials. Closed circuit television (CCTV) makes it possible for children with low vision to read print. The Optacon and Kurzweil reading machines make printed matter readily accessible to any blind student who can master their operation. However, reading devices are expensive and not uniformly available.

Closed Circuit Television.   Closed circuit television (CCTV) systems are electronic low-vision aids. They present high-contrast images of printed or written materials on a cathode ray monitor. Their principal advantage is that they allow students with various types of visual impairment, even those who are unable to read regular large print, access to print materials. The CCTV enlarges letter size according to the needs of the user, and contrast between letters and background can also be

Magnification through CCTV allows access to print material

adjusted. Even clearly drawn pictures and maps can be magnified. The material to be read is placed on a stand beneath or next to the monitor. Some models allow for a split screen or for print to be shown one line at a time. The models vary in size, but most are about the size of a small television set. There are several types of CCTVs on the market; some models can be attached to computers.

Anna, who was introduced in Chapter 6, had experienced many difficulties in learning to read. She could recognize single words but could not read sentences, even in a large-print reader. She was given a CCTV. In addition to making letter recognition much easier, the machine relieved Anna from having to set up a reading stand and fuss with the book; in essence, the CCTV motivated Anna to read. She progressed from reading single words and phrases to simple stories.

Eleven-year-old Joey had such extremely low vision that he had been diagnosed as being blind. An observant teacher noticed that Joey had good guiding vision for mobility and decided to introduce him to a CCTV. Joey, a braille user, had many problems with braille numbers and computations on the brailler. A CCTV simplified the process: Its high magnification allowed Joey to see the numbers on the screen, so he could write out his computations with a typewriter and see what he was writing on the monitor. The CCTV motivated Joey and encouraged his interest in doing mathematics.

The Optacon.   The Optacon (Optic to Tactile Converter) was developed at Stanford University as a reading device for the blind. It is a portable battery-operated machine that converts the image of a printed letter into a tactile impression. The unit is roughly the size of a large tape recorder and consists of a scanning camera module, the main electronic unit, and the tactile display. When the reader's left index finger is placed in position on the device, tiny vibrating pins that reproduce the shape of the letters read by the camera create tactile images that seem to float across the underside of the finger. There are several accessories available for the Optacon such as tracking aids, a battery charger, and a typewriter lens module.

Users require a period of concentrated training and practice in order to perceive the letters formed by the vibrating pins. The device is most useful to those who do not have physical handicaps. Users must have sufficient sensitivity in their fingers to be able to interpret the tactile impressions. A great deal of practice is required before efficient reading skill is attained.

Leanne was 16 years old when she lost functional use of her vision. Deaf at birth, she had normal sight until she was 13, when her vision began to deteriorate rapidly due to retinitis pigmentosa. By the time she was 20, Leanne had only a small amount of peripheral vision. Growing up as a deaf person, she had great difficulty adjusting to the loss of sight. Leanne never learned to speak; she communicated with sign language and two-handed British finger spelling. With the assistance of an interpreter and the aid of an Optacon and its typewriter attachments, Leanne is taking courses at a community college.

The Kurzweil Reading Machine.   The best-known example of an audio output reading device is the Kurzweil reading machine, developed at the Massachusetts Institute of Technology. The Kurzweil machine, produced by the Kurzweil Company of Cambridge, MA, consists of a scanner and electronic control units. An electronic voice "reads" the print material. The voice sounds artificial, but it is comprehensible and the rate of the speech output is adjustable. The reader controls the course of the reading process by turning the pages, aligning the text, and controlling reading speed (Jarkler, 1980). Unlike the Optacon, the Kurzweil machine depends on a computer to classify and identify the characters. The machine reads at a rate comparable to reading aloud.

These devices have a data base large enough to enable the text recognizer to perform well with all forms of printed matter, including book printing and typewriter text (Jarkler, 1980).

Communication Devices

Electronic technology is giving voice to those who cannot speak. Augmentative communication systems, discussed in Chapter 5, have been dramatically elaborated and expanded by electronic technology. For example, it has made communication boards more versatile and more adaptable to a variety of settings and situations. Nonspeaking people derive the greatest benefit from versatile equipment that doesn't confine or limit communication (Ring, 1980). Devices that offer few response options may restrict rather than expand the possibilities available to the user; as Ring noted, technology is a good slave but a poor master. Communication devices should be judged by the extent to which they encourage and enhance human relationships.

Communication needs vary from one individual to another and from one environment to another. As children grow, their needs change. As they acquire more skill in operating equipment, they must have available devices capable of adapting as well. Some systems are very limited in the options they provide; they may be able to transmit a few messages, but they cannot store, decode, or enhance. The Yes and No machine is an example of just such a device.

The Yes and No Machine.   The Yes and No machine is a flat board with two round buttons for Yes and No. When a button is pushed, an electronic voice announces a Yes or No. The board fits on the lap tray of a wheelchair. The child is only required to press the buttons in order to reply to questions. Similar devices may use synthetic speech to ask for "help," "a drink," or other requests. More complicated devices have a memory function so that the message may be prepared in advance.

Systems that can retrieve numerous already-coded messages are required for more natural and complex communicative interchanges. As computers become more frequently employed for communication, there is an increasing need for expert programmers who are aware of and sensitive to the needs of the handicapped community (Beukelman, Yorkston, & Dowden, 1985).

The Vidialog.   More sophisticated equipment is being designed for severely handicapped persons who cannot speak or use a typing machine, even one with an enlarged keyboard. One such device, the Vidialog, was described by Jarkler (1980). Produced in Denmark, the Vidialog uses an ordinary television display and can be adapted for people with different types of physical handicaps. Students capable of only a single movement will be able to operate it. The system, which works with a microcomputer, allows the user to direct the movement of a cursor that scans letters on a display monitor. The user must make three switch-operating movements to write each letter. The first starts the cursor, which vertically scans the display until the desired row is found. The second halts vertical movement and causes the cursor to move horizontally across the row. When the desired letter is reached, the third movement places it in the writing area of the screen (Jarkler, 1980). The Vidialog system can deliver large-size print.

Electronic Communication Boards. Personal electronic communication boards can be built to whatever size is needed and can be configured to operate automatically. Letters, words, phrases, sentences, or pictorial symbols may be used on a board. On some communication devices the messages are displayed on thin film overlays, so that the messages can be changed according to children's needs (Beukelman, Yorkston, & Dowden, 1985).

A scanning device is an essential part of the equipment. It scans the board to help the user locate the desired message. Scanning may be visual or auditory. Visual scans display all the possible selections (the menu). Audio scans require the user to memorize the menu in order to make a choice and are therefore slower than visual scanning.

Beukelman, Yorkston, and Dowden (1985) described the use of an auditory scanning device designed for a 17-year-old named David. Severe head injuries had left David blind, speechless, and paralyzed. Before computerized auditory scanning was introduced, David could only communicate with his parents, spelling out his requests in a time-consuming manner: His mother would recite the alphabet, and David would press on her arm with his thumb when she came to the letter he wanted. This slow and laborious process kept David dependent on personal contact with his communication partners. An audio scan system was designed that included pre-prepared phrases such as "I don't know," "Yes," "No," and "Please leave me alone." David also learned Morse code, using a thumb switch attached to the communication device to create the dots and dashes.

The Talking Word Board. A major advance in communication board systems is represented by the Talking Word Board (Beukelman,

Yorkston, & Dowden, 1985). The system is comprised of a keyboard, software, and an Apple II+ or IIe. The Unicorn Keyboard (Unicorn Engineering, Oakland, CA) and the Adaptive Firmware Card and Talking Word Board Program (produced by Adaptive Peripherals, Seattle, WA) are the components of the system.

The Talking Word Board has many advantages: It can be programmed in the setting in which it is to be used, and most of its functions can be tailored to individual needs. A set of display symbols can be placed on the membrane keyboard. The keys are large enough to permit the use of different types of symbol systems such as photographs, pictorial symbols, printed letters, or words. In addition, both a computer screen and a speech synthesizer can be utilized. The system is capable of providing messages that range from single letters to utterances of up to 40 characters. Other advantages are its potential for rapid communication with a variety of people. The communication partners do not have to understand the system; they need not look at the board. The board provides rapid feedback to the user and is adaptable to individual levels of motor and cognitive capacity. Its main disadvantage is that it is too bulky to be mounted on a wheelchair (Beukelman, Yorkston, & Dowden, 1985).

The Talking Data Terminal.   The Talking Data Terminal was developed as an aid for blind computer programmers and data terminal users (Jarkler, 1980). It can be connected to any type of terminal or modified to be used by itself. A special keyboard allows the user to move a cursor around on the terminal screen and find the section of interest. The Enhanced PC Talking Program (Computer Conversations, 1987) is a highly sophisticated system compatible with a variety of computers. Instead of typing, the user can command the computer system verbally, creating a two-way communication system between the computer and the user, thus making the equipment accessible to visually impaired students with physical handicaps. Current users range in age from 7 to 80. This equipment was designed by a blind programmer and is produced by Computer Conversations of Columbus, OH (Computer Conversations, 1987).

Communication Devices for Persons with Combined Vision and Hearing Impairments.   Combined vision and hearing impairments interfere with both the learning of language and ease of communication. The choice of mode of communication depends on a number of factors, such as degree of residual hearing and/or vision, age at onset of impairment, and communication styles employed before onset. As Kates and Schein

(1980) indicate, where one of these two senses retains more ability, communication via the more intact sense is preferred. There is great variation among this population.

Various communication devices are available that make it possible to send and receive messages, work with computers and even talk on the telephone. The Cybernetics Research Institute developed a two-way communication system called DEBLICOM (the Deaf-Blind Communication System). Information is transmitted kinesthetically and received in the form of palpable vibrations on the user's fingers. The machine uses a portable programming device. Additional output mechanisms can be incorporated into the DEBLICOM system, which has been adapted for Morse code and braille (Kates & Schein, 1980).

Two devices have been developed to enable the use of the telephone by people who have impaired vision and hearing but are able to speak: the Visual Speech Indicator and the Tactile Speech Indicator. The Visual Speech Indicator, a small portable device attached to a telephone receiver, can be used by persons who have some residual vision. Speaking into the phone, the visually/hearing impaired user asks questions that can be answered with "yes" and "no" by the party on the telephone line. "No," "yes," "please repeat," and "hold it" are the messages that the device can receive and translate into flashing lights. It takes about fifteen minutes to learn to use the system (Kates & Schein, 1980).

Like the Visual Speech Indicator, the Tactile Speech Indicator requires that the user ask yes/no questions. The device then amplifies the signals received and converts them into vibrations: one vibration for "yes," two for "no," and three for "please repeat." This device can also receive Morse code.

The Vibralert is an electronic signaling system that can be used as a doorbell or as a paging system. Carried in a pocket, the receiver transmits vibrations to the user as short pulses. The Vibralert is manufactured by Bell and Howell Communications Company.

The TAC-COM (Tactile Communication System) is a similar paging device that consists of a transmitter and one or more receivers that can be carried in a pocket. The receivers are powered by rechargeable batteries and vibrate when a signal is received (Kates & Schein, 1980).

Speech Aids. A bewildering variety of communication aids for speech-impaired people are currently available. Aids that improve speech, such as amplifiers for faint speech, mechanisms that produce artificial voice, and maskers for stammering are used by people who cannot produce clear or audible speech. Prosthetic aids can support speech with amplification or screen out speech hesitations such as severe stammering. These aids offer an alternative for those whose handicaps interfere with speech production (Ring, 1980).

Tools for Living

The term "tools for living" describes prosthetic devices designed to permit disabled people to function as independently as possible (Wolff, 1980). Tools for living are technical devices that include aids for cleaning, dressing, and feeding oneself, wheelchairs, standing boards, and equipment to be used in the kitchen and bathroom. Like other adaptive equipment, their purpose is to enhance personal functioning and interaction. Electronic technology has the potential of improving the devices currently available.

New technology has enormously improved the quality of prostheses and other types of technical rehabilitation aids. Speech aids have been mentioned. It is beyond the scope of this book to discuss all forms of rehabilitation equipment. However, it is important to note that appropriate equipment, combined with knowledge of how to use and maintain it, can create and enrich opportunities for participation and independence. Further information about the varieties of technical tools for living may be obtained from Abledata, a computerized listing of commercially available products for rehabilitation and independent living. This information is available from the National Rehabilitation Information Center (NARIC), 4407 Eighth Street N.E., Washington, DC 20017.

Problems and Issues in the Development and Distribution of Electronic Aids

Wolff (1980) suggested that tools for living should be as ordinary and acceptable as other work tools and obtainable through ordinary commercial channels. Accessibility is curtailed because many of these devices can only be obtained on prescription as medical appliances, rather than simply as tools to enhance living. Tools for living are the same as other tools; they extend the physical capacities of users (Wolff, 1980).

Other factors that affect the design and distribution of technical aids include the attitudes of family and school personnel and the degree to which a climate of acceptance is created. The social acceptability of aids sometimes makes the difference in their use. Malone (1980) noted that a great deal can be done to make aids more attractive in the public view. For example, eyeglasses have discarded their "aid" image. They are now perceived as "fashionable" and are designed as accessories. This contrasts with hearing aids, which are still not completely socially acceptable.

The design of technical aids is another important issue. More and quicker communication is needed between engineers and consumers. Those who do the research and marketing should be acquainted with the particular needs of handicapped individuals.

Teachers need to become familiar with technology and learn to be at ease with its presence in the classroom. As a myriad of unsuccessful attempts to implement educational technology has demonstrated, systems fail when teachers are not comfortable with and able to operate technical equipment. Technical aids that support independence must be easy to operate and must not be detrimental to residual function. They must be reliable and easy to set up by the teacher, aide, or therapist (Soede, 1980).

There is a pressing need for research, evaluation, and dissemination of information about available equipment. Manufacturers interested in producing technical aids would do more design and development if they had the financial resources to do so. In some countries there are government programs that encourage the design and manufacture of technical aids. For example, the Swedish Institute for the Handicapped has the resources to initiate research and development and the Swedish government provides disabled people with appropriate technical aids free of charge (Lindstrom, 1980).

Technical aids are being produced in all technically advanced countries. An international forum to serve as a clearinghouse of information and support for research and development would go a long way toward solving problems of dissemination across international boundaries (Uyttendale, 1980). Governments, universities, and public and private health and social agencies have an important role to play in the research, manufacture, and distribution of expensive equipment. One of the brightest promises of sophisticated technology is its power to draw attention toward the assets and resources of disabled people and away from an emphasis on disability.

Summary

The promise of technology resides in its capacity to provide a means of achieving independent interaction, and in many areas this promise is being fulfilled. Interface mechanisms exist in sufficient variety and adaptability to allow even the most severely impaired individuals to work with computers. Output devices such as speech synthesizers provide immediate feedback and offer new possibilities for communication with other people. Computer technology has made a wide range of devices available to enable nonspeaking individuals to communicate with their environments; the most advanced of these devices are flexible and can be designed to meet highly individual needs. Complementing these communication systems are tools for living, a variety of technical aids to enhance independence and participation.

The full capabilities of technology will never be realized by relying solely on the efforts of engineers and technicians. Teachers working with technology must be sophisticated in using it and able to select appropriate software. Financial and organizational resources must be committed to overcoming the current state of affairs in which access to the new equipment is limited by cost, methods of production and distribution, and dissemination of information. Finally, society must learn to see the various devices not as markers of disability, but as doors of opportunity, for the communication they make possible operates in two ways: It opens up the world to handicapped people, and it enriches the world by allowing them to participate and contribute.

The Normalization of Experience

Normalization implies that handicapped individuals are accorded the same rights and opportunity for cultural participation available to other members of society. Social policies capable of translating normalization principles into programs and services make the most enduring gains when they are rooted in the principles of human development (Zigler & Muenchow, 1980). The concept of normalization, the belief that the living and learning environments of handicapped children should reflect the norms of society, was introduced in Chapter 1. The social interests of children extend beyond the statement of principles into the realities of experience. This chapter deals with the social tasks of education, with school environments, social learning, integration into community schools, and living and working in the community. Serving the social interests of children enhances their social identities as full-fledged participants of school and society. The social identities of children reflect the quality of their interactions within their homes and schools and within society at large.

The Social Interests of Children and Their Families

Continuity gives meaning to experience and relationships. In the lives of children, continuity resides in ongoing relationships with their families. Zigler and Muenchow (1980) emphasize the importance of continuity in all stages of the lives of children. As children move from infancy through childhood to adulthood, the experience of continuity gives meaning to growth. Early intervention is important, but so is preparation for adult life in the community. Coordination and integration of family support service systems helps to make continuity a reality in children's lives. In too many jurisdictions, public policy as it affects children with complex handicaps is formulated and carried out without regard to this principle (Zigler & Muenchow, 1980).

When public policymakers lose sight of the importance of the family, well-intentioned concepts such as normalization and integration are in danger of becoming empty slogans. Parents attempting to solve the sometimes overwhelming problems of care imposed by serious handicaps need a framework of societal supports as much as their children do. It is not enough to consider only the special compensatory services; human needs also must be considered in the provision of social and educational services.

The Concerns of Parents

A chief concern of parents is knowing how to find and gain access to services for their children. Frustration, anguish, and even desperation are the lot of many parents seeking services for their children. Human services such as infant intervention programs, special needs preschools, special education programs, and postsecondary training are inconsistently or poorly funded, fragmented among several different agencies, and sometimes nonexistent. When agencies serving the visually impaired are unable to serve the needs of children who have other disabilities as well, parents must turn to other agencies, such as those serving physically or mentally handicapped children, that are also unable to meet all needs of their children. National agencies are beginning to recognize the importance of networking and coordination of services. In recognition of the fragmentation and difficulty of accessing services, a national center for networking was established in the United States.

Another source of concern to parents is the way in which services are sometimes defined. For example, children with special health needs or those who cannot move independently from wheelchair to bed are considered "pediatric extended care" in some communities. This means they have no access to community-based schools or other community services. In some jurisdictions, children need to be public wards before they can receive special and expensive services (Zigler & Muenchow, 1980). When services are denied, parents often have no way of challenging or appealing denial of service (British Columbians, 1986).

Service plans that focus only on special needs frustrate the deepest needs of parents wanting to maintain involvement in decisions affecting the lives of their children. Lord (1985) pointed out that scarce resources can more effectively address human needs when planning is coherent, flexible, and includes parents or other caregivers in decision making.

Rigid planning and funding systems pose "a significant barrier to really seeing and knowing the people we serve. Since one form of service often dominates, this is also one of the ways that service systems maintain social monopolies" (Lord, 1985, p. 1).

Zigler and Muenchow (1980) suggest that public policy should empower parents to make decisions about the best placements for their children. New types of services focus on strengthening the role of the family. Children receive tremendous benefits from intervention programs designed to assist parents to work with their own children, rather than leaving all forms of treatment to the professionals (Goodson & Hess, 1975).

Resources for Families

Family training centers are a relatively new resource for families. Some of these centers are community based, others have been located on the grounds of residential institutions. These centers provide training for the parents and involve them in assessment and educational planning for their children.

Some state and private residential schools for the blind are attempting to fill gaps in services by offering diagnostic and family support services. These schools are building close ties with the children's home communities. For example, the Arizona School for the Blind offers educational diagnostic services to children, their families, and their home communities. Children and their families come to live at the school for a short period for observation and evaluation. Recommendations are made to the schools in their home communities. Teachers from the Arizona school go to the home schools to monitor children's progress and provide additional suggestions as needed.

Social Interests in Assessment and Diagnosis

Parental hopes are dashed when they are faced with uncaring and rigid professional attitudes. They cannot help feeling that their children's abilities are minimized when professionals do not consider their own accounts or opinions of their children's abilities. When decisions about children's futures rest on negative and thoughtless assessments, there is cause for concern.

With difficult-to-assess children, it is important to consider the opinions of people who know the child well. In general, intimate relationships with even the most damaged children lead to more positive assessments of abilities than nonintimate clinical studies (Goode, 1984). Yet clinical, nonintimate interactions sometimes determine how and where children will live, what kind of education or training they may receive, and even, on occasion, whether they will live or die (Goode, 1984).

Children with complex handicaps can only be meaningfully evaluated by clinical procedures that take place in familiar settings. Evaluation is an ongoing process and cannot be separated from treatment. It is important that examiners have knowledge of how to adapt testing and evaluation materials for use with visually impaired students. Distractability, behavioral outbursts, and attempts to throw materials or leave the assessment situation can be minimized when procedures are modified. For example, sitting next to or behind blind children in order to guide their hands through an expected response is a comfortable way of showing them what is required (Langley, 1986).

The way physically handicapped students are positioned often makes a great difference in their ability to respond. Children who do not have head control should be positioned so that they can coordinate their eyes and hands. Stabilizing the shoulder or providing support to the arm and hand encourages nonverbal students to use their hands to point, write, or otherwise manipulate materials. This type of support often makes the difference between getting an appropriate response and no response at all (Langley, 1986).

Some children require a warm-up period before they can be tested; others can maintain concentration for only short periods of time. Knowing the student enables the examiner to know when to pick up or slow down the rate of presentation (Langley, 1986). The aims of evaluation are to identify children's abilities in relation to their disabilities. Abilities, not disabilities, provide realistic bases for educational planning.

Nonspeaking children with little motor control have no way of showing their abilities until some mode of expression can be developed. Lack of motor control should never be assumed to preclude mental ability, comprehension of language and ideas, or capacity to learn to read and write. The social interests of children are poorly served when severe handicaps are equated with severe and profound mental retardation.

Mimi, who was discussed in Chapter 4, illustrates that high levels of cognitive function can exist side by side with severe visual and motor impairments. When her parents first agreed to have her participate in a study of communication skills of multiply handicapped children, Mimi was nonverbal, unable to hold her head or use her hands, and difficult to assess. Her parents identified several areas that they felt expressed Mimi's awareness of other people. Mimi greeted her father every night with a long stream of vocal sounds, as if she were telling him the news of the day, and consistently vocalized when her mother sang to her, as if she were trying to sing.

Mimi responded well to intervention. With support to her hand, 7-year-old Mimi is learning to read and do simple arithmetic. She has learned to spell, write clearly, remember sequences of numbers and letters, make letter/sound associations, spell words, and generate sentences and phrases.

Nonspeaking children who display unusual talent in art or music may not receive the attention they deserve. The term "idiots savants" is frequently used to describe individuals who show remarkable talent in one area. It is always safer to consider artistic or musical abilities as indications of mental potential, rather than to view them as isolated phenomena.

The importance of considering talent as a predictor of broader capability rather than as an isolated and unrelated oddity can be seen in the case of Jamie, a nonverbal 12-year-old partially sighted boy. Encephalitis when he was 2 years old left him with partial sight, a moderate hearing loss, expressive language difficulties, and a motor disability. Jamie draws extremely well; his portrayals of animals are exquisite in detail, and alive with color and movement. His mother thought that he could not draw so well unless he perceived visual forms and color and protested when Jamie was placed in a segregated school for "severely handicapped" children.

Jamie's mother complained to the principal: "We take him to the zoo and he comes home and draws every animal he has seen." Jamie's parents refused to accept the school's evaluation and persuaded the principal to arrange for Jamie to attend an art class in a nearby elementary school. With an adapted easel placed on the tray of his wheelchair Jamie participated in the art class with children of his age. The art teacher was impressed by Jamie's work. He showed him how to work with paints and charcoal. "Jamie's art communicates for him," the art teacher commented. His handicaps are irrelevant to his participation in an art class. Jamie was moved to a special class within the school, where he learned to operate a computer.

The Social Tasks of Education

The ultimate aims of education are social and personal competence. Social competence is social intelligence. Gardner (1983) hypothesized that intelligence is complex and manifest as different types of "intelligences." For example, the mental operations required for object-related and spatial skills differ from verbal and other language-related abilities. Social intelligence is a domain of its own. The personal or social forms of intelligence reflect the influences of culture and society. Like language and play skills, social skills are acquired in the course of social interactions with both adults and peers. Social knowledge is shaped by society and revolves about interpersonal relationships (Gardner, 1983). Social intelligence is expressed by social knowledge, social problem solving, and awareness of the needs and feelings of other people. The perception and interpretation of social cues and social problem solving depend on social knowledge (Davies & Rogers, 1985).

Rosen, Clark, and Kivitz (1977) distinguish between social knowledge and social skills. Social skills are based on social knowledge and encompass cultural conventions (manners) and the ability to communicate cooperative and empathetic responses to other people. Compliance and obedience are sometimes confused with cooperation. Compliance may simply be a response to social pressure; cooperation is a conscious desire to please other people.

There is a strong relationship between social experience and social competence. Children who experience happy and satisfying interactions with loving adults learn to find deep rewards in reaching outside of themselves. Children who feel denied or rejected learn to reject in turn. While self-reliance and independence are important parameters of social adjustment, they do not stand alone. There are handicapped individuals who attend school or work programs, dress and feed themselves, purchase their own clothing, and stay out of trouble, but who are still socially withdrawn, lonely, uncomfortable in social settings, and generally unhappy (Rosen, Clark, & Kivitz, 1977). Social adjustment factors have a greater bearing than intelligence does on the success of adjustment to community life (Rosen, Floor, & Baxter, 1971).

Self-Esteem and School Environments

The social identities of children reflect the perceptions of significant others. Salzinger, Antrobus, and Glick (1980) suggest that feedback from the environment is the most important characteristic of ecosystems. The ecosystem is comprised of all the interactions children have with their environments. Environments have profound effects on self-identity. When children feel valued and accepted by others, they are more likely to value and accept themselves (Tuttle, 1987).

The interactions between the interpersonal and intrapersonal factors engender the sense of self in society (Gardner, 1983). The intrapersonal factors include self-identity, which has to do with how children learn to regard themselves. According to Tuttle, the judgments children make about themselves reflect the opinions of others. Children with handicaps are likely to receive inconsistent and mutually incompatible reflections from significant adults. In Tuttle's view (1987), there are four hurdles to be overcome by handicapped children in their pursuit of self-esteem. The first is the problem of acquiring coping skills. The second is learning to maintain self-esteem in the face of negative reflections. The third is being able to perceive alternatives and make choices. The fourth hurdle is learning how to deal with the problems associated with their dependence on other people.

School environments have a profound effect on the way children come to perceive themselves. Controlling and restricted environments teach children that they have little control over their lives. Overprotective and oversheltering environments promote ''helplessness'' because they teach children to do nothing. Helplessness is a pattern of inertia acquired during years of overprotection and oversheltering (Rosen, Clark, & Kivitz, 1977). Overly dependent children learn to help themselves by manipulating others to meet their needs. The following anecdote would be amusing were it not so poignant.

Sixteen-year-old Denise was difficult to motivate. Her considerable abilities were dormant beneath her stubborn and negative refusal to do anything at school. Her parents, deeply saddened by her handicap, never came to terms with her blindness. They felt sorry for her and looked after her every need. Denise had no responsibilities at home and refused responsibility at school. She turned her energies to avoiding work, even when it was simpler to do it. One day, her teacher insisted that she learn to make a sandwich. Denise refused and no amount of coaxing would move her. Exasperated, her teacher asked, ''What will you do when you are grown up?''

''I'm going to get married and have a family,'' Denise replied.

''How will you take care of your children if you won't even know how to make a sandwich?'' her teacher asked.

''Oh,'' said Denise, ''I'll have volunteers.''

Truly helpless people have no systematic ways of meeting their own needs. They experience all environmental occurrences, positive or negative, as beyond their control. From a social learning point of view, educational environments are as important as curricula in teaching children social skills. Deep-seated habits of noninvolvement are the product of unstimulating and unresponsive environments. Low frequencies of adult/child interaction allow behavior patterns to develop in nonsystematic ways (Oswin, 1978). The ignored child does not seek attention and caregivers and teachers cease to think that the child needs attention (Beail, 1985). Knowing how to obtain adult attention in school situations is a learned behavior.

It is sometimes difficult to distinguish between emotional problems and simply not understanding what is expected. Patterns of passivity, dependency, submissiveness, low self-esteem, attention-seeking, and inertia present major problems to school adjustment. Emotional problems and maladjustment among these children tend to be wholly attributed to their handicaps, when the source of difficulty may be the environment. Like other people, handicapped children develop emotional problems when they are in conflict with their environments and have high levels of frustration and anxiety. As Salzinger, Antrobus, and Glick (1980) point out, analysis of children's interactions with their environments reveals how the context in which disturbed behavior occurs may serve to strengthen and maintain disturbed and disturbing behavior.

For example, Jeanine had many tantrums in the special preschool she attended. Whenever she screamed, the teachers removed her from the room and sat her in a favorite chair, a rocking chair in a separate room. Screaming became Jeanine's way of asking to go to the rocking chair. Responsive and stimulating environments encourage interaction and bring children into contact with other people.

Opportunities for interactions with one's peers are a necessary component in learning the social skills of the peer culture. The most compelling argument for mainstreaming and integration is found in the opportunities for social interaction provided by integrated community schools.

Mainstreaming

Schools reflect the attitudes, values, and social policies of the larger society. The social struggle for acceptance of handicapped people in society is expressed by the growing movement advocating integration of all handicapped children into community schools.

Parent efforts to obtain access to appropriate education for their children resulted in the "Education for All Children Act" (U.S. Public Law 94-142). This act clearly mandates that children with severe handicaps receive a free and appropriate education in the least restrictive environment. The notion of "least restricted environment" implies that children be placed in school settings that allow maximum access to normal childhood experiences. In other words, to the greatest extent possible, handicapped children should be educated with nonhandicapped peers.

Public policy in both Canada and the United States encourages the integration of handicapped children into public elementary and high schools. The delivery of special education services varies with the policies of individual school districts, the laws of states and provinces, the extent of available specialized services, and the philosophies of school principals. Mainstreaming has been interpreted in various ways by different school districts. In some places, there have been efforts to integrate severely handicapped students within graded classes with extra assistance; in others integration is the inclusion of special classes within the public school. Integration may be achieved for portions of the school day or it may be complete, depending on students' special needs.

An increasing number of mainstreamed or integrated models of special education indicate that highly specialized services can be offered in nonspecialized settings. For example, in Brookline, Massachusetts, there is a model program at one elementary school. The school has a resource room where the students with special needs go for activities such as physical therapy and other individualized programs (Gurry, 1986). Nonhandicapped children come to the resource room to be peers/buddies with handicapped children.

Small-group interaction is usually most effective; it encourages positive interactions and teaches nonhandicapped children to accept and include severely handicapped peers in daily activities. Nonhandicapped children learn to offer help only when it is needed. The success of the Brookline program is due to the degree of planning and teamwork among the teachers, therapists, and principal. Potentially, the experience of these children will contribute to the acceptance of disabled people by society at large (Gurry, 1986).

Mainstreaming policies allow for a continuum of educational plans. Placement is generally determined by the amount of specialized education instruction needed. Mainstreaming plans allow for complete or partial integration. Having a continuum of services offers the flexibility to adjust to the needs of individual children throughout their school careers. The continuum consists of:

Regular classroom
Regular class + support teachers
Regular class + resource room
Part-time placement in a special needs class

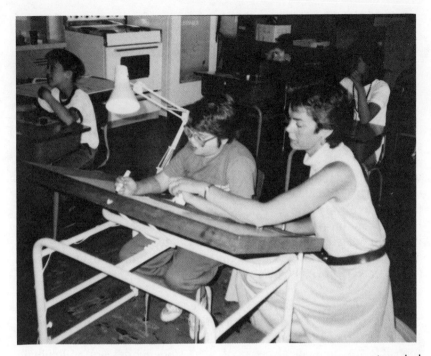

Adapting the environment can be as simple as including an appropriate desk and light in a regular classroom

Full-time special class
Special day school

Mainstreaming has changed the delivery of educational services and is creating new opportunities for handicapped children and their teachers. The outstanding features of mainstreaming are that it:

Takes place in public school environments
Permits children to receive specialized programs
Permits modifications to regular curriculum
Encourages new roles for special education teachers, such as consultant and/or itinerant roles
Unites the skills of regular and special educators
Requires the cooperation of school administrators, parents, special educators (including teachers for the visually impaired), classroom teachers, aides, and other personnel
Involves parents in educational planning for their children

Depends for success on the formulation of individual education plans that summarize educational goals and describe procedures for reaching them, reflecting the schools' and the parents' expectations for the child

Includes outreach programs for children with special medical needs

Partial Integration.   Resource room programs are one type of partial integration particularly suited for children with visual handicaps. Resource rooms, located in public elementary and secondary schools, provide specialized instruction such as braille reading and writing, low vision skills, orientation and mobility instruction, and use of special equipment. The children are enrolled in regular classes and come to the resource room for part of every day or several days each week. Flexible and individualized programs permit resource rooms to serve visually impaired children with a variety of learning problems. Partial integration may also take the form of participation in regular classes for particular subjects, such as music, art, or homemaking.

Itinerant Programs.   By providing the specialized instruction and adapting school materials, itinerant teachers enable children to have success in integrated programs. In itinerant programs, teachers responsible for the special needs of their students develop individualized programs and close working relationships with other classroom teachers. In many smaller communities, the itinerant teacher is the only resource person for visually impaired children. Ideally, caseloads should be small enough to permit these teachers to devote the time and resources needed.

Teacher Education.   The attitudes and expectations of teachers are a critical element in the success of community-based services. Such attitudes and expectations are typically acquired during university preparation. Sarason and Doris (1978) pointed out that while public policy calls for placing handicapped children in integrated settings, teacher training programs have made few adaptations or changes in their curricula. Most university preparation programs in special education are defined in terms of disability categories. This has led to fragmentation and competition within the profession. Generic systems, intended to avoid the proliferation of disability categories by classifying by degree of handicap rather than type, have many advantages. These systems employ the terms "mild," "moderate," and "severe" to classify children. However, generic classifications may obscure the special educational needs of children with visual impairments.

Teachers preparing to work with visually impaired children should be knowledgeable about the interactive effects between visual problems and other disabilities. Likewise, teachers preparing to serve mentally handicapped individuals need an understanding of the impact of sensory impairments. All teachers serving handicapped children need to understand the philosophical and legal premises underlying the integration movement.

Developmental concepts lose their meaning when they are reduced to simplistic categories and characteristics. For example, some children may not speak until they are 7 or 8 years old, but their comprehension of language may be age appropriate. Appreciation of the dynamics of growth and learning, an inventory of skills and methods, ability to work with colleagues and administrators to "get things done for children," and an abiding faith in children's ability to learn are the characteristics of well-prepared teachers.

Planning for Social Interaction. In integrated settings there are both formal and informal opportunities for peer group interactions. In segregated environments, children, especially those who are nonverbal, have no opportunities to hear peer-speech or practice communication skills. Communication between children may be as simple as a smile, a laugh, or a jaunt around the playground. Carefully planned peer/buddy/tutor systems create a climate in which friendships develop. Small-group interactions and informal playtimes offer plentiful opportunity for interaction. Careful planning contributes to the success of interaction, as can be seen in the following example.

It is recess time, and Tony, an 8-year-old child who is both blind and physically handicapped, is outside on the playground with his classmates. Tony is waiting for his friend, Jimmy, a robust third grader. Tony smiles as he hears Jimmy call out to him. "Hey, do you want a ride?" Jimmy asks. Tony grins, nods his head, and laughs. "Okay," says Jimmy, pushing the wheelchair. "Hold on tight, we're off."

In this case, the third graders had been prepared to be peer/buddies by their teacher. The special class teacher was invited to their room to talk with them about her students. She gave simple explanations about her students and their handicaps, answered questions, and invited the third graders to be special friends to her students. Jimmy volunteered to be a special friend to Tony and came to play with Tony at recess time.

In mainstream settings, there are many ways to increase opportunities for interaction. Special classrooms located in central locations within school buildings and planned interactions within the frame-

Integration can succeed even with severely impaired children

work of school routines provide physical and organizational structures that promote peer group interaction.

Social Interests and the Curriculum

The social tasks of education serve the human as well as special needs of children. The specialized aspects of curriculum have been discussed in other chapters. Personal competence is nourished by experiences that enrich and cultivate imagination and creativity and bring children into contact with the world at large.

Next to the home, the school is the social environment where children spend most of their time. Flexible school environments and age-appropriate curricula and materials allow for flexibility and individual progress. There is growing evidence that materials and activities that reflect students' chronological ages, rather than developmental ages, lessen the stigma of being handicapped (Bates, Morrow, Pancsofar, & Sedlak, 1984).

The creative arts, drama, puppetry, music, and dance reach deep inside the child and draw expressiveness out. Art experiences bring children into intimate contact with materials that yield to the fingers. Sculpting in clay appeals to the sense of touch and gives blind children a medium they can explore, control, and create in (Fukurai, 1969). Adapted physical education and outdoor activities bring children in contact with the larger community. Reading and writing increase in importance when they become tools of expression as well as indicators of academic achievement.

Handicapped children require more input, more experience, and more time. Providing opportunities to put skills to work, slowing down the tempo of instruction, and taking the time to teach them how to organize their desks and learning materials contribute to the efficiency of learning. When children try to do things for themselves, they signal their readiness to assume responsibility. As M. Donaldson (1978) pointed out, school experience should provide the ways and means through which children can discover their abilities and interests and realize themselves in the joys of achievement and learning.

Transitions To Adulthood

Life after the school years undergoes an abrupt change for many young people. Visually impaired students, especially those with developmental handicaps, graduate from school with no idea of how to spend the rest of their lives. School programs suddenly cease when they turn 18, 19, or 21. Chronological age, not maturity, determines when students leave school.

Surveys indicate that despite previous participation in special education programs, the majority of visually impaired developmentally handicapped young adults have major problems in bridging the gap from school to community living and work. Transitions programs are being developed to enable successful transition from school to the community.

Successful participation in the community requires that young adults perform a wide variety of personal management tasks, have skills needed in the workplace, and be able to participate in recreational and leisure activities. Transitions programs, developed at the secondary level, incorporate living skills such as shopping for clothing and groceries, using public transportation, learning about money, and maintaining a checkbook, as well as prevocational and vocational skills. Cooperation and involvement of students' families and service agencies contribute to the success of transitions programs (Haring & Billingsley, 1984).

Community Employment

A network of activities and services provides the supportive structure of successful community programs. Planning for transitions ideally begins before the student is 16 years old. At the outset, information regarding transition and employment goals should be made available to the student's parents. A major goal of transition planning is the identification of the type of work an individual is able to do and the adaptations and support services that may be required (McDonnell & Hardman, 1985). Real-life work experiences in shops, restaurants, or factories allow students to make meaningful employment choices.

Project ADVANCE, an innovative program for deaf-blind young people, was developed at the Perkins School for the Blind in 1980. The purpose of the project is to enable students to explore and experience paid employment on a part-time basis while they are still in school. Work sites include competitive employment, student-operated small businesses, sheltered enclaves within industry, and sheltered employment (Roberts, Huebner, & Simpson, 1987).

The responsibilities of teachers involved in Project ADVANCE are divided into three phases. The first is to provide active training in job tasks and related work behaviors and social skills in the workplace. Once that has been accomplished, the teachers transfer supervisory responsibility to the employer/supervisor. Thereafter, teachers maintain contact and assist with problems that may arise in the workplace.

Success as a student does not ensure success as an employee. Students often lose jobs because they have poor work habits and attitudes. Identification and development of work skills while the students are still in school ensures greater success in community-based work programs.

Traditional work-training systems may not be appropriate for young adults who require more support and follow-up. The Rehabilitation Research and Training Center at Virginia Commonwealth University developed a model of supported employment for persons with severe disabilities. The goal is paid employment in regular integrated work situations, not sheltered workshops. Program directors advocate "Experience first, training second" (Roberts, 1987).

Another type of supported work option is enclaves/work crews in industry. Work crews are supervised at all times. The supported work approach requires highly structured job placements, individualized on-site training, and job retention skills. This model has been successfully implemented by both public school and community service organizations (Roberts, Huebner, & Simpson, 1987). Supported employment is suitable for those who are not ready for competitive employment. Experience has shown that students with good knowledge of life skills and satisfactory orientation and mobility succeed in both community living and vocational placements.

Postschool Living-Skills Centers

Community-based programs have been referred to as "service stations with the purpose of enhancing the will and the way to self-determination" (Weiner, 1986, p. 20). Living-skills programs incorporate life skills, mobility training, and other personal adjustment skills. Living skills are best taught in the situations they are needed. Some living skills centers operate in conjunction with residential programs. The Living Skills Center in Contra Costa County, California, provides experience in independent apartment-type living, social and personal management skills, and orientation and mobility. The Therapeutic Living Skills Center, near Pasadena, California, is a residential program designed for visually impaired young people with developmental difficulties. It provides training in orientation and mobility, personal and family counseling, and recreational activities.

Sex Education

Sex education is an important aspect of functional curricula aimed at enhancing and developing the social identities of children. As Neff (1982) has indicated, the rights of impaired persons to function as full and complete human beings must include being informed about sexual matters. The issue of the school's responsibility in teaching about sexuality is fraught with controversy, yet children who are denied access to important information about themselves cannot fully realize themselves as normal human beings. Sex education does not only deal with the physiological aspects of reproduction. Sexuality concerns gender identification, awareness of oneself as male or female, awareness of the opposite sex and what makes them different, management of menstruation, sexual feelings, and awareness of culturally appropriate sexual behavior.

Self-identity is not completely possible without knowing one's gender. Knowledge of gender differences is difficult for blind children in the absence of explicit and honest instruction. Anatomical differences between male and female can be taught with the use of realistic models. Some commercially manufactured dolls, such as Little Brother and Sister produced by Creative Playthings, provide the required details. Neff (1982) also suggests that cut-out figures, department store mannequins, and statues can be utilized to develop awareness of body characteristics. Allowing children to explore clothing, such as bras and men's underwear, provides additional opportunities to reinforce concepts of gender (Neff, 1982). As realistic concepts are developed, further information about sexual intercourse, masturbation, and the reproductive process should be provided in consultation and cooperation with children's families.

Residential Services

As children grow into adulthood, it is normal that they move away from their homes and families and form relationships outside of the family circle. Options in residential programs have greatly increased and include supervised group homes and supervised apartment living. Settings in which two or three handicapped adults live together provide socially interesting, normal living experiences. Residential arrangements for young adults with multiple handicaps include:

Living independently, with supervision by social worker or community nurse

Minimal support units, where a small number of handicapped people live together

Group homes serving five to eight persons and staffed by residential counselors

Hostels

Short-term residential arrangements to permit the families of younger children to go on holidays or simply give the families relief from care are also needed. Respite care may be supplied by:

Short-term foster care or family support schemes. The handicapped child lives with another family for varying periods of time.

Short-term care in special hostels maintained by the state, province, or local associations such as associations for the physically or mentally handicapped.

Short-term care hospitals. These are for the most severely handicapped children, who may be difficult to manage in homes not equipped for their physical care.

Children in Institutions

Carole, a blind and physically handicapped child, was placed in a large residential institution when she was 9 years old. She lived on a ward for severely and profoundly handicapped children because of the level of care she required. With little stimulation and few activities, Carole withdrew into silence. An occupational therapist was attracted to the silent child and spent time talking and playing with her. When asked why she never spoke, Carole explained, "I didn't have anyone to talk to. The other kids couldn't talk and the nurses had to feed, dress and bathe all of us kids. They never had time to sit and talk. Sometimes I talked to myself in whispers at night. I guess that's why I didn't forget how to talk."

While public policy is advocating integration and community placement, many hundreds of children and young adults still live in large residential institutions. Severely handicapped children, children without families, and those whose families are unable to cope with their care continue to be served in state and provincial institutions.

The most suitable environments for children are family-type living units. Children's wards should be administered as autonomous homes, staffed by permanent caregivers independent of the institution administration (Oswin, 1978; Mortimore & Mortimore, 1985). Home-like small units administered by housemothers are preferable to ward-type arrangements. Educational and rehabilitation programs such as communication training and orientation and mobility should be incorporated into daily routines.

There is an important role for volunteers in the lives of institutionalized children. Retired people and other volunteers provide friendship and personalized care that is missing from the lives of many children. The Volunteer Grandparent Program in place in many state institutions is deeply enriching the lives of many children and adults. For very young children there is no substitute for home care. Children who cannot live with their own families should, wherever possible, be placed in foster homes where they can receive the quality of personalized attention they need in order to thrive.

Summary

This chapter has addressed the social interests of children and their families. These social interests are served only when service providers consider the children's human needs along with their special needs. The education and habilitation of children with complex needs is ongoing. The need for specialized services does not end with adolescence. Transition programs, continuing education in community colleges, and vocational placements contribute to continuity and quality of life. Social policies that reflect the developmental needs of children for continuing relationships with their families and communities give meaning to concepts of normalization. Providing families with the resources to maintain their children and ensure the delivery of needed services requires coordination and integration of services at the community level. The quality of community-based service makes the policies and principles of normalization and integration a reality in the lives of children and their families.

Afterword

The aims of this book have been to 1) clarify, identify, and portray the human consequences of complex handicaps, 2) to synthesize research and show its applications to a unified approach to intervention, and 3) to illustrate educational interventions designed to encourage and develop social and environmental interaction. By most estimates, more than half of all blind and visually impaired children have additional developmental handicaps. In addition, many children with neurological handicaps have undiagnosed visual problems that cause learning difficulties. Labels such as multiply handicapped, severely handicapped, and so forth tend to obscure the real needs of the children and their families. Such labels create low expectations and deny access to appropriate educational and treatment services. Severe visual handicaps, especially when they occur in association with neurological, orthopedic, and/or hearing handicaps, disguise potential by robbing children of the resources for efficient learning. The learning problems of many children are a direct consequence of their inability to access sources of information and participate in interaction. Understimulation, passivity, and noninvolvement profoundly affect the ways they come to perceive themselves and the world around them. Responsive environments and adults who believe in their abilities to learn and to grow make it possible for these children to develop personal competence and master the skills of living.

Research in such fields as infant and language development is clarifying the role of adults in mediating learning. The chapters on early intervention, sensorimotor development, and language and communication have drawn on this research and illustrated its application to educational interventions. Encouraging children to participate, interact, and learn to cope with the demands of living is an ongoing lifetime process. No single intervention and no stage of development is more important than any other. Living successfully demands a range of supportive and educational services from infancy through adulthood. The journey towards personal fulfillment begins with the knowledge that one is capable of interacting with and influencing the actions of other people. Therefore, the first goal of educational intervention is to invite the participation of the child.

Education in its truest sense endows experience with significance. Meaning and a sense of social identity are acquired through thousands of encounters with the social and physical world. Confidence and self-reliance are shaped in the course of activities and experiences in every domain of learning, be it sensorimotor, language, or acquiring the skills of independent living. Learning is multifaceted and interrelated. Participation and involvement can be achieved with structured interaction. Motivation comes with knowing that one is capable of interacting and of influencing events. The methods that have been described and illustrated achieve their aims with careful identification of desired outcomes and an appreciation of the developmental process. As children begin to participate and become involved with their environments, progress in one domain is generalized to others. Educational goals are realized with the emergence of self-motivated individuals who willingly and eagerly seek interaction in their dealings with the world around them.

References

Als, H., Tronick, E., & Brazelton, T. B. (1980). Stages of early behavioral organization: The study of a sighted infant and a blind infant in interaction with their mothers. In T. M. Field, S. Goldberg, D. Stern, & A. M. Sostek (Eds.), *High risk infants and children* (pp. 181–203). New York: Academic Press.

Assaf, A. A. (1982). The sensitive period: Transfer of fixation after occlusion for strabismus amblyopia. *British Journal of Ophthalmology, 66* (1), 64–70.

Ayres, A. J. (1972). *Sensory integration and learning disorders*. Los Angeles: Western Psychological Services.

Balzarini, J. (1979). *Randy*. Unpublished manuscript, University of British Columbia, Faculty of Education, Vancouver.

Barraga, N. (1964). *Increased visual behavior in low vision children*. New York: American Foundation for the Blind.

Barraga, N. (1976). *Visual handicaps and learning*. Belmont, CA: Wadsworth Publishing.

Bates, E. (1979). Intentions, conventions, and symbols. In E. Bates, L. Benigni, I. Bretherton. L. Camaioni, & V. Volterra (Eds.), *The emergence of symbols: Cognition and communication in infancy* (pp. 33–50). New York: Academic Press.

Bates, P., Morrow, S. A., Pancsofar, E., & Sedlak, R. (1984). The effect of functional vs. non-functional activities on attitudes/expectations of non-handicapped college students: What they see is what we get. *Journal of the Association for Persons with Severe Handicaps, 9* (2), 73–78.

Bauman, M. K., & Yoder, N. M. (1966). *Adjustment to blindness—Reviewed*. Springfield, IL: Charles C. Thomas.

Beail, N. (1985). The nature of interactions between nursing staff and profoundly multihandicapped children. *Child: Care, Health and Development, 11* (2), 105–112.

Benton, A. (1979a). Body schema disturbances: Finger agnosia and right-left disorientation. In K. M. Heilman & E. Valenstein (Eds.), *Clinical neuropsychology* (pp. 141–156). New York: Oxford University Press.

Benton, A. (1979b). Visuoperceptive, visuospatial, and visuoconstructive disorders. In K. M. Heilman & E. Valenstein (Eds.), *Clinical neuropsychology* (pp. 186–219). New York: Oxford University Press.

Berg, B. B. (1975). Convulsive disorders. In E. E. Bleck & D. A. Nagel (Eds.), *Physically handicapped children: A medical atlas for teachers* (pp. 101–108). New York: Grune & Stratton.

177

Bersani, H., Jr. (1987). Center provides timely answer to family support questions. *TASH Newsletter, 13* (1), 4.

Beukelman, D. R., Yorkston, K. M., & Dowden, P. A. (1985). *Communication augmentation: A casebook of clinical management.* San Diego, CA: College Hill Press.

Bloom, L. (1973). *One word at a time: The use of single word utterances before syntax.* The Hague: Mouton.

Bobath, B. (1985). *Abnormal postural reflex activity caused by brain lesions,* 3rd edition. London: Heinemann.

Boxill, E. H. (1985). *Music therapy for the developmentally disabled.* Rockville, MD: Aspen Systems Corporation.

Brady, M. P., & Cunningham, J. (1985). Living and learning in segregated environments: An ethnography of normalization outcomes. *Education and Training of the Mentally Retarded, 20* (4), 241–251.

Brazelton, T. B. (1977). *Infants and mothers: Differences in development.* New York: Delacorte Press.

Bricker, R. P., & Lewis, M. (1982). Co-occurrence and intervention. *Topics in Early Childhood Special Education, 2* (2), 1–16.

British Columbians for Mentally Handicapped Persons. (1986). *Parent Brief.* Unpublished manuscript.

Bronfenbrenner, U. (1975). Is early intervention effective? In B. Z. Friedlander, G. M. Sterritt, & G. E. Kirk (Eds.), *Exceptional infant: Assessment and intervention* (vol. 3, pp. 449–475). New York: Brunner/Mazel.

Brown, R. (1973). *A first language: The early stages.* Cambridge, MA: Harvard University Press.

Bruner, J. S. (1966). *Learning about learning: A conference report.* Washington, DC: Department of Health, Education, and Welfare.

Bruner, J. (1983). *Child's talk: Learning to use language.* Oxford: Oxford University Press.

Bruner, J. S., & Sherwood, V. (1976). Peek-a-boo and the learning of rule structures. In J. S. Bruner, A. Jolly, & K. Sylva (Eds.), *Play—Its role in development and evolution* (pp. 244–261). New York: Penguin.

Budoff, M., Thormann, J., & Gras, A. (1984). *Microcomputers in special education.* Cambridge, MA: Brookline Books.

Bullowa, M. (1979). Prelinguistic communication: A field for scientific research. In M. Bullowa (Ed.), *Before speech: The beginning of interpersonal communication* (pp. 1–49). Cambridge, England: Cambridge University Press.

Byrne, M. E. & Shervanian, C. C. (1977). *Introduction to communication disorders.* New York: Harper & Row.

Chukovsky, K. (1968). *From two to five.* Berkeley: University of California Press.

Chukovsky, K. (1976). The sense of nonsense verse. In J. S. Bruner, A. Jolly, & K. Sylva (Eds.), *Play—Its role in development and evolution* (pp. 596–602). New York: Penguin.

Clarke, A. M., & Clarke, A. D. B. (1979). Early experience: Its limited effect upon later development. In D. Shaffer & J. Dunn (Eds.), *The first year of life: Psychological and medical implications of early experience* (pp. 135–152). New York: Wiley.

Cogburn, L. (1979). *Maria*. Unpublished manuscript, University of British Columbia, Faculty of Education, Vancouver.

Colenbrander, A. (1976). Low vision: Definition and classification. In E. E. Faye (Ed.), *Clinical low vision* (pp. 3–6). New York: Little, Brown.

Computer Conversations. (1987) *Interactive solutions: The one that works* [brochure]. Columbus, OH: Computer Conversations.

Connor, F. P., Williamson, G. G., & Siepp, J. M. (1978). *Program guide for infants and toddlers with neuromotor and other developmental disabilities*. New York: Teachers College Press.

Corn, A. (1983). Visual function: A theoretical model for individuals with low vision. *Journal of Visual Impairment and Blindness, 77* (9), 373–377.

Cratty, B. J., & Sams, T. A. (1968). *The body-image of blind children*. New York: American Foundation for the Blind.

Croce, R. V., & Jacobson, W. H. (1986). The application of two-point touch cane technique to theories of motor control and learning implications for orientation and mobility training. *Journal of Visual Impairment and Blindness, 80* (6), 790–794.

Crystal, D. (1976). *Child language, learning and linguistics*. London: Edward Arnold.

Curtin, B. (1976). Visual acuity in myopia. In E. E. Faye (Ed.), *Clinical low vision* (pp. 295–300). New York: Little, Brown.

Davies, E. (1984). Communication supplements: Perspectives on usage. In D. Muller (Ed.), *Remediating children's language: Behavioral and naturalistic approaches* (pp. 158–171). San Diego, CA: College Hill Press.

Davies, R. R., & Rogers, E. S. (1985). Social skills training with persons who are mentally retarded. *Mental Retardation, 23* (4), 186–196.

DeLaguna, G. A. (1963). *Speech: Its function and development*. Bloomington: Indiana University Press. (Original work published 1927)

Denhoff, E. (1979). Medical aspects. In W. Cruickshank (Ed.), *Cerebral palsy: A developmental disability* (pp. 29–72). Syracuse, NY: Syracuse University Press.

Dent-Cox, T. (1985). *Sensorimotor rhymes*. Unpublished manuscript.

deVilliers, P. A., & deVilliers, J. G. (1978). *Language acquisition*. Cambridge, MA: Harvard University Press.

Donaldson, J. (1980). Changing attitudes toward handicapped persons: A review and analysis of research. *Exceptional children, 46* (7), 504–514.

Donaldson, M. (1978). *Children's minds*. Glasgow, Scotland: Fontana/Collins.

Elgie, J. (1979). *Tracy*. Unpublished manuscript, University of British Columbia, Faculty of Education, Vancouver.

Elliott, J. M., & Connolly, K. J. (1984). A classification of manipulative hand movements. *Developmental Medicine and Child Neurology, 26* (3), 283–295.

Emde, R. (1978). *The prerepresentational self and its affective core*. Paper presented at the Chicago Institute of Psychoanalysts.

Eyde, D. R., & Menolascino, F. J. (1981). Prescriptive play as a prelude to maximizing personality growth among the severely handicapped. *Viewpoints in Teaching and Learning, 57*(1), 74–81.

Faulk, J. P. (1985). *Adapting toys to facilitate language development in handicapped preschoolers*. Unpublished manuscript.

Faye, E. E. (1976a). Clinical definition and classification of the low vision patient. In E. E. Faye (Ed.), *Clinical low vision* (pp. 7–14). New York: Little, Brown.

Faye, E. E. (1976b). Management of the child. In E. E. Faye (Ed.), *Clinical low vision* (pp. 329–342). New York: Little, Brown.

Feitelson, D., & Ross, G. S. (1973). The neglected factor–Play. *Human Development, 16* (3), 202–223.

Fellows, R. R., Leguire, L. E., Rogers, G. I., & Bremer, D. I. (1986). A theoretical approach to vision stimulation. *Journal of Visual Impairment and Blindness, 80*(8), 907–908.

Fewell, R. R. (1983). Assessing handicapped infants. In S. G. Garwood & R. R. Fewell (Eds.), *Educating handicapped infants: Issues in development and intervention* (pp. 257–291). Rockville, MD: Aspen Systems.

Field, T. (1983). High-risk infants "have less fun" during early interactions. *Topics in Early Childhood Special Education, 3*(1), 77–87.

Fraiberg, S. (1977). *Insights from the blind: Comparative studies of blind and sighted infants*. New York: Basic Books.

Fraiberg, S. (1979). Blind infants and their mothers: An examination of the sign system. In M. Bullowa (Ed.), *Before speech: The beginning of interpersonal communication* (pp. 149–170). Cambridge: Cambridge University Press.

Fromkin, V. A., Krashen, S., Curtiss, S., Rigler, D., & Rigler, M. (1974). The development of language in Genie: A case of language development acquired beyond the critical period. *Brain and Language, 1* (1), 81–107.

Fukurai, S. (1969). *How can I make what I cannot see?* New York: Van Nostrand.

Gardner, H. (1983). *Frames of mind: The theory of multiple intelligences*. New York: Basic Books.

Gardner, J. M., & Karmel, B. Z. (1982, March). *Neonates' arousal level and visual attention to temporal frequencies*. Paper presented at the International Conference on Infant Studies, Austin, TX.

Garvey, C. (1977a). *Play*. Cambridge, MA: Harvard University Press.

Garvey, C. (1977b). The contingent query: A dependent act in conversation. In M. Lewis, & L. A. Rosenblum (Eds.), *Interaction, conversation, and the development of language* (pp. 63–93). New York: Wiley.

Garwood, S. G. (1983). Physical development in infancy. In S. G. Garwood & R. R. Fewell (Eds.), *Educating handicapped infants: Issues in development and intervention* (pp. 71–112). Rockville, MD: Aspen Systems.

Gerstmann, J. (1958). Psychological and phenomenological aspects of disorders of the body image. *Journal of Nervous and Mental Diseases 126*(6), 499–512.

Gilbert, D., Finell, L., & Young, R. (1978). Young children's awareness of self. *Psychological Reports, 43* (3), 911–914.

Gold, M. (1980). *Try another way.* Champaign, IL: Research Press.

Goldberg, S. (1977). Social competence in infancy: A model of parent-infant interaction. *Merrill-Palmer Quarterly, 23*(3), 163–178.

Goode, D. E. (1984). Socially produced identities, intimacy, and the problem of competence among the retarded. In L. Barton & S. Tomlinson (Eds.), *Special education and social interests* (pp. 228–248). Beckenham, England: Croom Helm.

Goodson, B. D., & Hess, R. D. (1975). *Parents as teachers of young children: An evaluative review of some contemporary concepts and programs.* (ERIC Document Reproduction Service No. ED 136 967)

Green, K. (1986). *Prosthetics and adaptive equipment.* Unpublished report, Massachusetts Department of Mental Health.

Greenfield, P. M., & Smith, J. H. (1976). *The structure of communication in early language development.* New York: Academic Press.

Gross, V., & Melzack, R. (1978). Body image: Dissociation of real and perceived limbs by pressure cuff ischemia. *Experimental Neurology, 61*(3), 680–688.

Guldager, V. (1970). *Body Image and the severely handicapped rubella child* (Perkins Publication No. 27). Watertown, MA: Perkins School for the Blind.

Gurry, S. (1986). Noah's school: Integration works in Brookline. *TASH Newsletter 12*(12), 6.

Haith, M. M. (1980). *Rules that babies look by: The organization of newborn visual activity.* Hillsdale, NJ: Lawrence Erlbaum Associates.

Hall, A. (1982). Teaching specific concepts to visually handicapped students. In S. Mangold (Ed.), *A teacher's guide to the special educational needs of blind and visually handicapped children* (pp. 10–19). New York: American Foundation for the Blind.

Halliday, M. A. K. (1975). *Learning how to mean: Explorations in the development of language.* London: Edward Arnold.

Hammer, E. (1984). *The quality of life for multihandicapped blind and visually impaired infants, children and youth.* Paper presented to Helen Keller Seminar, American Foundation for the Blind.

Haring, N., & Billingsley, F. F. (1984). Systems-change strategies to ensure the future of integration. In N. Certo, N. Haring, & R. York (Eds.), *Public school integration of severely handicapped students: Rational issues and progressive alternatives* (pp. 153–167). Baltimore, MD: Paul Brookes.

Harley, R. K., & Lawrence, G. A. (1977). *Visual impairment in the schools.* Springfield, IL: Charles C. Thomas.

Hart, V. (1984). Research as a basis for assessment and curriculum for visually impaired infants. *Journal of Visual Impairment and Blindness, 78*(7), 314–318.

Hass, J. (1985). *Vision enhancement and the multiply handicapped child.* Unpublished manuscript.

Herron, R., & Sutton-Smith, B. (1971). *Child's play.* New York: Wiley.

Hill, P. M., & McCune-Nicolich, L. (1981). Pretend play and patterns of cognition in Down's syndrome children. *Child Development, 52*(2), 611–617.

Hill, E., & Ponder, P. (1976). *Orientation and mobility techniques: A guide for the practitioner.* New York: American Foundation for the Blind.

Hobbs, N. (1980). An ecologically oriented, service-based system for the classification of handicapped children. In S. Salzinger, J. Antrobus, & J. Glick (Eds.), *The ecosystem of the "sick" child* (pp. 271–290). New York: Academic Press.

Hrncir, E. J. (1985). Infant play: A window to motivational competence. In J. L. Frost & S. Sunderlin (Eds.), *When children play: Proceedings of the international conference on play and play environments* (pp. 339–342). Wheaton, MD: Association for Childhood Education International.

Hyvarinen, J., & Hyvarinen, L. (1982). Higher functions and plasticity in visual pathways. In L. Hyvarinen & E. Lindstedt (Eds.), *Early visual development: Normal and abnormal (Acta Ophthalmologica Supplement 157).*

Immamura, S. (1965). *Mother and blind child.* New York: American Foundation for the Blind.

Isenberg, J., & Jacobs, J. (1982). *Playthings as learning tools: A parent's guide.* New York: Wiley.

Itard, J. M. G. (1972). Report on the progress of Victor of Aveyron. In L. Malson (Ed.), *Wolf children and the problem of human nature.* New York: Monthly Review Press. (Original work published 1806)

Jabbour, J. T., Duenas, D. A., Gilmartin, R. C., Jr., & Gottlieb, M. I. (1976). *Pediatric neurology handbook* (2nd ed.). Flushing, NY: Medical Examination Publishing.

Jarkler, B. (1980). Communication aids for various handicaps. In J. Bray & S. Wright (Eds.), *The use of technology in the care of the elderly and handicapped: Tools for living* (pp. 83–92). Westport, CT: Greenwood Press.

Jose, R. T., Smith, A. J., & Shane, K. G. (1980). Evaluating and stimulating vision in the multiply impaired. *Journal of Visual Impairment and Blindness, 74*(1), 2–8.

Kagan, J. (1981). *The second year: The emergence of self-awareness.* Cambridge, MA: Harvard University Press.

Kalveboer, A. F. (1979). Neurobehavioral findings in pre-school and school-aged children in relation to pre- and perinatal complications. In D. Shaffer, & J. Dunn (Eds.), *The first year of life: Psychological and medical implications of early experience* (pp. 55–68). New York: Wiley.

Kates, L., & Schein, J. D. (1980). *A complete guide to communication with deaf-blind persons.* Silver Spring, MD: National Association for the Deaf.

Keller, H. (1955). *Teacher: Anne Sullivan Macy.* New York: Doubleday (Dolphin Books).

Kellogg, R. (1963). *Analyzing children's art.* Palo Alto, CA: National Press.

Kinney, W. B. (1979). The relationship of body image and perceptual motor performance. *International Journal of Rehabilitation Research, 2*(2), 225–232.

Kirk, S. A., & Gallagher, J. J. (1979). *Educating exceptional children.* Boston: Houghton Mifflin.

Knoll, J., & Ford, A. (1987). Community participation must be goal of in-home services. *TASH Newsletter, 12*(1), 1, 4.

Kreiser, M. (1979). *Anna.* Unpublished manuscript, University of British Columbia, Faculty of Education, Vancouver.

Kronheim, J. K. (1985). *Learning pillows and other friends* [brochure]. 17 Chaske Ave., Auburndale, MA: author.

Landau, B. (1983). Blind children's language is not "meaningless." In A. E. Mills (Ed.), *Language acquisition in the blind child* (pp. 62–76). San Diego, CA: College Hill Press.

Langley, B. B. (1986). Psychoeducational assessment of visually impaired students with additional handicaps. In D. Ellis (Ed.), *Sensory impairments in mentally handicapped people* (pp. 253–297). San Diego, CA: College Hill Press.

Lemeshow, S. (1982). *The handbook of clinical types of mental retardation.* Boston: Allyn and Bacon.

Lenneberg, E. H. (1967). *Biological foundations of language.* New York: Wiley.

Leonard, L. B. (1982). Early language development and language disorders. In G. Shames & E. H. Wiig (Eds.), *Human Communication Disorders* (pp. 221–257). Toronto: Charles E. Merrill.

Linder, T. W. (1982). Pleasurable play: Its value for handicapped infants and their parents. *The Journal for Special Educators, 19*(1), 59–68.

Lindstrom, J. I. (1980). Providing aids for the handicapped—A multifunctional process. In J. Bray & S. Wright (Eds.), *The use of technology in the care of the elderly and the handicapped: Tools for living* (pp. 238–241). Westport, CT: Greenwood Press.

Lord, J. (1985). Human service planning: Neglected or co-opted? *Centre News Report* (Kitchner, Ontario, Centre for Research and Education in Human Service), *2*(1), 1.

Lowenfeld, B. (1981). Effects of blindness on the cognitive functions of children. In B. Lowenfeld (Ed.), *On blindness and blind people: Selected papers* (pp. 67–78). New York: American Foundation for the Blind. (Original work published 1948)

McConkey, R. (1984). The assessment of representational play: A springboard for language remediation. In D. J. Muller (Ed.), *Remediating children's language: Behavioural and naturalistic approaches* (pp. 113–134). San Diego, CA: College Hill Press.

McCord, W. T. (1983). The outcome of normalization: Strengthened bonds between handicapped persons and their communities. *Education and Training of the Mentally Retarded, 18*(3), 153–157.

McDonnell, J., & Hardman, M. (1985). Planning the transition of severely handicapped youth from school to adult services: A framework for high school programs. *Education and Training of the Mentally Retarded, 20*(4), 275–286.

MacDowell, J. H. (1979). *Children's riddling.* Bloomington: Indiana University Press.

McKay, D. (1985). A theory of the representation, organization and timing of action with implications for sequencing disorders. In E. A. Roy (Ed.), *Neuropsychological studies of apraxia and related disorders* (pp. 267–308). New York: North Holland (Elsevier Science Publishers).

McLean, J. E., & Snyder-McLean, L. K. (1978). *A transactional approach to early language training.* New York: Merrill.

McLean, J., & Snyder-McLean, L. K. (1984). Recent developments in pragmatics: Remedial implications. In D. J. Muller (Ed.), *Remediating children's language* (pp. 55–82). San Diego, CA: College Hill Press.

MacNamara, J. (1972). Cognitive basis of language learning in infants. *Psychological Review 79*(1), 1–13.

Magnet, J. E., & Kluge, E. M. W. (1987). *Withholding treatment from defective newborn children.* Quebec: Brown Legal Publications.

Malone, J. F. (1980). An aid to the definition of "aids." In J. Bray & S. Wright (Eds.), *The use of technology in the care of the elderly and the disabled: Tools for living* (pp. 5–13). Westport, CT: Greenwood Press.

Mellor, D. (1979). Hereditary syndromes associated with neurological disorder and early visual handicaps. In V. Smith & J. Ken (Eds.), *Visual handicap in children* (Clinics in developmental medicine. No. 73, pp. 102–111). London: William Heinemann.

Moores, D. F. (1978). *Educating the deaf: Psychology, principles and practices.* Boston: Houghton Mifflin.

Mortimore, J., & Mortimore, P. (1985). How should policy makers develop institutions for the future? *Child: Health, Care and Development, 11*(5), 267–280.

Mysak, E. D. (1976). *Pathologies of speech systems.* Baltimore, MD: Williams and Wilkins.

Mysak, E. D. (1980). *Neurospeech therapy for the cerebral palsied: A neuroevolutional approach.* New York: Teachers College Press.

Napier, J. R. (1976). *The human hand.* Burlington, NC: Scientific Publications Division, Carolina Biological Supply Company.

Neff, J. (1982). Sexuality education methodology. In S. S. Mangold (Ed.), *A teacher's guide to the special educatinal needs of blind and visually handicapped children* (pp. 63–71). New York: American Foundation for the Blind.

Nickel, B. L., & Hoyt, C. S. (1982). The hypoxic retinopathy syndrome. *American Journal of Ophthalmology, 93*(5), 589–593.

Nirje, B. (1969). The normalization principle and its human management implications. In R. Kugel & W. Wolfensberger (Eds.), *Changing patterns in residential services for the mentally retarded* (pp. 179–195). Washington, DC: President's Committee on Mental Retardation.

Nordoff, P., & Robbins, C. (1985). *Therapy in music for handicapped children*. London: Victor Gollancz.

Ornstein, R., & Thompson, R. F. (1984). *The amazing brain*. Boston: Houghton Mifflin.

Oswin, M. (1978). *Children living in long-stay hospitals*. London: William Heinemann Medical Books.

Packer, M., & Rosenblatt, D. (1979). Issues in the study of social behavior in the first week of life. In D. Shaffer & J. Dunn (Eds.), *The first year of life: Psychological and medical implications of early experience* (pp. 7–36). New York: Wiley.

Piaget, J. (1958) *The child's construction of reality*. London: Routledge and Kegan Paul.

Piaget, J. (1962). *Play, dreams, and imitation in childhood*. New York: W. W. Norton.

Piaget, J., & Inhelder, B. (1969). *The psychology of the child*. New York: Basic Books.

Ring, N. D. (1980). Communication aids for the speech impaired. In J. Bray & S. Wright (Eds.), *The use of technology in the care of the elderly and the handicapped: Tools for living* (pp. 79–82). Westport, CT: Greenwood Press.

Roberts, F. K., Huebner, K. M., & Simpson, F. (Eds.). (1987). *Collaborative planning: Transition from school to work*. New York: American Foundation for the Blind.

Robinson, P. (1975). *An educational approach utilizing developmental sequencing and co-active movement theory*. Lansing, MI: Department of Public Instruction.

Rogers, C. (1961). *On becoming a person*. Boston: Houghton-Mifflin.

Rogers, S. J., & Puchalski, C. B. (1984). Development of symbolic play in visually impaired young children. *Topics in Early Childhood Special Education, 3*(4), 57–63.

Rogow, S. M. (1981a). The appreciation of riddles by blind and visually handicapped children. *Education of the Visually Handicapped, 13*(1), 4–10.

Rogow, S. M. (1981b). Developing play skills and communicative competence in multiply handicapped young people. *Journal of Visual Impairment and Blindness, 75*(5), 197–203.

Rogow, S. M. (1982). Rhythms and rhymes: Developing communication in very young blind and multihandicapped children. *Child: Care, Health and Development, 8*(4), 249–260.

Rogow, S. M. (1987). The ways of the hand: Hand function in blind, visually impaired, and visually impaired multihandicapped children. *British Journal of Visual Impairment, 5*(2), 59–62.

Rose, S. A. (1983). Behavioral and psychological sequelae of pre-term birth: The neonatal period. In T. Field & A. Sostek (Eds.), *Infants born at risk: Physiological, perceptual, and cognitive processes* (pp. 45–68). New York: Grune and Stratton.

Rosen, M., Clark, G. R., & Kivitz, M. S. (1977). *Habilitation of the handi-*

capped: New dimensions in programs for the developmentally disabled. Baltimore, MD: University Park Press.

Rosen, M., Floor, L., & Baxter, D. (1971). The institutional personality. *British Journal of Mental Subnormality, 17*(2), 2–8.

Rowland, C. (1984). Preverbal communication of blind infants and their mothers. *Journal of Visual Impairment and Blindness, 78*(7), 297–302.

Rubin, K. H. (1980). Fantasy play: Its role in the development of social skills and social cognition. *New Directions For Child Development: Children's Play, 9,* 69–85.

Rudel, R. (1978). Neuroplasticity: Implications for development and education. In J. S. Chall & A. F. Mirsky (Eds.), *Education and the brain.* (77th Yearbook of the National Society for the Study of Education, pp. 269–307). Chicago: University of Chicago Press.

Sacks, O. (1984). *A leg to stand on.* London: Gerald Duckworth.

Sacks, O. (1985). *The man who mistook his wife for a hat and other clinical tales.* New York: Summit Books.

Salzinger, S., Antrobus, J. & Glick, J. (1980) The ecosystem of the 'sick' kid. In S. Salzinger, J. Antrobus, & J. Glick (Eds.), *The ecosystem of the "sick" child* (pp. 1–18). New York: Academic Press.

Sangorvin, J. (1977). The "corporeal scheme" and motor deficiency. *Anuario de Psicologia, 16*(1) 95–111.

Sarason, S., & Doris, J. (1978). Mainstreaming: Dilemmas, opposition, opportunities. In M. E. Reynold (Ed.), *Futures of education for exceptional students: Emerging structures* (pp. 3–40). Minneapolis: National Support Systems Project, University of Minnesota.

Schantz, F. C. (1969). *Perceptual and cognitive aspects of body experience.* New York: Academic Press.

Schultz, T. R. (1974). Development of the appreciation of riddles. *Child Development, 45*(1), 100–105.

Seeley, W. S., & Thomas, J. E. (1966). Is mobility feasible with multiply handicapped blind children? *Exceptional Children, 32*(9), 613–618.

Seltzer, G. B. (1983). Systems of classification. In J. L. Matson & J. A. Mulick (Eds.), *Handbook of mental retardation* (pp. 143–156). New York: Pergamon Press.

Sigman, M. D. (1983). Individual differences in infant attention: Relation to birth status and intelligence at five years. In T. Field & A. Sostek (Eds.), *Infants born at risk: Physiological, perceptual and cognitive processes* (pp. 271–294). New York: Grune and Stratton.

Silverman, H., McNaughton, S., & Kates, B. (1978). *Handbook of blissymbolics.* Toronto: Blissymbolics Communication Institute.

Soede, M. (1980) Development and evaluation of complex aids. In J. Bray & S. Wright (Eds.), *The use of technology in the care of the elderly and the handicapped: Tools for living* (pp. 83–92). Westport, CT: Greenwood Press.

Sonksen, P. M. (1982). The assessment of vision for development in severely visually handicapped babies. In L. Hyvarinen & E. Lindstedt (Eds.), *Early* visual development: Normal and abnormal (Acta Ophthalmologica Supplement 157, pp. 82–90).

Sparrow, J. (1986). Case study in mobility. Unpublished manuscript, Faculty of Education, University of British Columbia, Vancouver.

Stephens, B., & Grube, C. (1982). Development of Piagetian reasoning in congenitally blind children. Journal of Visual Impairment and Blindness, 76(4), 133–143.

Stern, D. (1977). The first relationship: Infant and mother. Cambridge, MA: Harvard University Press.

Sutton-Smith, B. (1971). Child's play: Very serious business. Psychology Today, 5(7), 67–87.

Sylva, K. J., Bruner, J., & Genova, P. (1976). The role of play in the problem-solving of children 3–5 years old. In J. S. Bruner, A. Jolly, & K. Sylva (Eds.), Play: Its role in development and evolution (pp. 244–261). New York: Basic Books.

Tait, P. E. (1972). A descriptive analysis of the play of young blind children. Education of the Visually Handicapped, 4(1), 12–15.

Tait, P. E., & Ward, M. (1982). The comprehension of verbal humor by visually impaired children. Journal of Visual Impairment and Blindness, 76(4), 144–147.

Tallents, C. (1979). The visual handicaps found in a population of mentally and physically handicapped children. In V. Smith & J. Keen (Eds.), Visual handicaps in children (Clinics in Developmental Medicine No. 73, pp. 68–75). London: William Heinemann.

Tinbergen, N., & Tinbergen, E. A. (1983). Autistic children: New hope for a cure. London: Allen and Unwin.

Towbin, A. (1981). Neuropathological aspects: Perinatal brain damage and its sequels. In P. Black (Ed.), Brain dysfunction in children: Etiology, diagnosis and management (pp. 47–78). New York: Raven Press.

Trevarthen, C. (1979). The psychobiology of speech development. Neurosciences Research Program Bulletin, 12(4), 570–585.

Trevarthen, C. (1980). The foundations of intersubjectivity: Development of interpersonal and cooperative understanding in infants. In D. R. Olson (Ed.), The social foundations of language and thought: Essays in honor of Jerome S. Bruner (pp. 316–341). New York: W. W. Norton.

Tronick, E. (1981). Infant communicative intent: The infant's reference to social interaction. In R. E. Stark (Ed.), Language behavior in infancy and early childhood (Johnson and Johnson Round Table IV, pp. 5–39). New York: Elsevier.

Tronick, E., & Adamson, L. (1980). Babies as people: New findings on our social beginnings. New York: Collier Books.

Tubiana, R., Thomine, J. M., & Mackin, E. (1984). Examination of the hand and upper limb. Philadelphia: M. B. Saunders.

Tuttle, D. W. (1987). The role of the special education teacher-counselors in meeting student's self-esteem needs. Journal of Visual Impairment and Blindness, 81(4), 156–161.

Twitchell, T. E. (1970). Reflex mechanisms and the development of prehension. In K. Connolly (Ed.), *Mechanisms of motor skill development* (pp. 25–37). New York: Academic Press.

Uyttendale, D. (1980). The distribution of aids for the disabled. In J. Bray & S. Wright (Eds.), *The use of technology in the care of the elderly and the disabled: Tools for living* (pp. 262–267) Westport, CT: Greenwood Press.

Vandenberg, B. (1980). Play, problem-solving, and creativity. *New Directions For Child Development: Children's Play, 9,* 49–68.

Van der Heyden, A. H. C. (1979). *Shortterm visual information forgetting or what is forgotten in visual information processing and what was forgotten in visual information processing research.* Leiden: Rijksuniversiteit.

Van der Velde, C. D. (1985) Body images of one's self and of others: Developmental and clinical significance. *American Journal of Psychiatry, 142*(5), 527–537.

Van Dijk, J. (1968, May). *Movement and communication with rubella children.* Talk given at the Annual General Meeting of the National Association for Deaf-Blind and Rubella Children.

Van Dijk, J. (1982). *Rubella handicapped children: The effects of bilateral cataract and/or hearing impairment on behavior and learning.* Lisse, The Netherlands: Swets and Zeitlinger, B. V.

Van Hasselt, V. B., & Hersen, M. (1981). Applications of single case designs to research with visually impaired individuals. *Journal of Visual Impairment and Blindness, 75*(9), 359–362.

Vietze, P. M., McCarthy, M., McQuiston, S., MacTurk, R., & Yarrow, L. (1983). Attention and exploratory behavior in infants with Down's syndrome. In T. Field & A. Sostek (Eds.), *Infants born at risk: Physiological, perceptual and cognitive processes* (pp. 251–270). New York: Grune and Stratton.

Von Raffler-Engel, W. (1981). Developmental kinesics: The acquisition and maturation of conversational non-verbal behavior. In B. L. Hoffer & R. N. St. Clair (Eds.), *Developmental kinesics: The emerging paradigm* (pp. 5–23). Baltimore: University Park Press.

Walker, J. A., & Crawley, S. B. (1983). Conceptual and methodological issues in studying the handicapped infant. In S. G. Garwood & R. R. Fewell (Eds.), *Educating handicapped infants: Issues in development and intervention* (pp. 25–63). Rockville, MD: Aspen Systems.

Warburg, M., Fredericksen, P., & Ratleff, J. (1979). Blindness among 7700 mentally retarded children in Denmark. In V. Smith & J. Keen (Eds.), *Visual handicap in children* (Clinics in Developmental Medicine No. 73, pp. 56–67). London: William Heinemann.

Warren, D. (1984). *Blindness and early childhood development* (2nd ed.). New York: American Foundation for the Blind.

Watson, J. S. (1972). Smiling, cooing, and the "the game." *Merrill-Palmer Quarterly, 18*(2) 323–339.

Weiner, F. (1986). *No apologies: A guide to living with a disability, written by the real authorities—People with disabilities, their families and friends.* New York: St. Martin's Press.

Wells, C. G. (1981). *Learning through interaction: The study of language development*. New York: Wiley.

Wertsch, J. V. (1979). From social interaction to higher psychological processes: A clarification and application of Vygotsky's theory. *Human Development, 22*(1), 1–15.

Whitt, J. K., & Prentice, N. M. (1977). Cognitive processes in the development of children's enjoyment and comprehension of joking riddles. *Journal of Developmental Psychology, 13*(2) 129–136.

Williams, H. G. (1983). *Perceptual and motor development*. Englewood Cliffs, NJ: Prentice-Hall.

Wills, D. M. (1968). Problems of play and mastery in the blind child. *British Journal of Medical Psychology, 41* (Part 3), 213–222.

Wolfensberger, W. (1972). *Normalization: The principle of normalization in human services*. Toronto: Leonard Crainford Publisher.

Wolff, H. S. (1980). Introduction. In J. Bray & S. Wright (Eds.), *The use of technology in the care of the elderly and disabled: Tools for living* (pp. 3–5). Westport, CT: Greenwood Press.

Wolff, R. H. (1981). Discussion of social development and communicative behavior in infancy. In R. E. Stark (Ed.), *Language behavior in infancy and early childhood* (Johnson and Johnson Round Table IV, pp. 63–68). New York: Elsevier.

Woodcock, C. (1974). *Blind children who function on a retarded level*. New York: American Foundation for the Blind.

Yakura, C. (1986). *Case study in mobility*. Unpublished manuscript, Faculty of Education, University of British Columbia, Vancouver.

Yarrow, L. J., Morgan, G. A., Jennings, K. D., Harmon, R. J., & Gaiter, J. L. (1982). Infants' persistence at tasks: Relationships to cognitive functioning and early experience. *Infant Behavior and Development, 5*(1) 131–141.

Zigler, E., & Muenchow, S. H. (1980). Principles and social policy implications of a whole-child psychology. In S. Salzinger, J. Antrobus, & J. Glick (Eds.), *The ecosystem of the "sick" child* (pp. 239–249). New York: Academic Press.

Zigler, E., & Trickett, P. K. (1978). I.Q., social competence and evaluation of early childhood intervention programs. *American Psychologist, 33*(9), 789–798.

Index

About the Author

SALLY M. ROGOW is Professor in the Department of Educational Psychology and Special Education and Director of the Diploma Program in the Education of Children with Visual Impairments at the University of British Columbia. In addition to giving frequent lectures and workshops on the education of visually impaired children, Dr. Rogow has written widely for professional journals and has edited and co-authored special education publications for provincial and state agencies in Canada and the United States.